When I Was a Boy

WHEN I WAS A BOY

Scenes and Stories from My Childhood

Ruskin Bond

Illustrated by Sunaina Coelho

TALKING CUB

Published by Speaking Tiger Publishing Pvt. Ltd
4381/4 Ansari Road, Daryaganj, New Delhi-110002, India

Published in Talking Cub by Speaking Tiger in hardback in 2018
Copyright © Ruskin Bond 2018
Illustrations copyright © Sunaina Coelho 2018

ISBN: 978-93-88326-61-2
eISBN: 978-93-88326-60-5

10 9 8 7 6 5 4 3 2 1

The moral right of the author has been asserted.

Typeset in Lora by Jojy Philip
Printed at Sanat Printers, Kundli

All rights reserved.
No part of this publication may be reproduced, transmitted,
or stored in a retrieval system, in any form or by any means,
electronic, mechanical, photocopying, recording or otherwise,
without the prior permission of the publisher.

This book is sold subject to the condition that it shall not, by way
of trade or otherwise, be lent, resold, hired out, or otherwise
circulated, without the publisher's prior consent, in any form of
binding or cover other than that in whichit is published.

Contents

1.	Raise the Curtains	7
2.	Beware of the Lion!	19
3.	Aeroplanes, Laddoos and Orange Pips in My Stomach	29
4.	Walks with Daddy	44
5.	The Room of Many Colours	61
6.	Wars and Mad Kings	76
7.	The Wrestlers	92
8.	The Tunnel of Friendship	119
9.	Books and Friends	144
10.	Magic Eggs	158
11.	A Boy's Own Room	171
	Epilogue	187

~ 1 ~

Raise the Curtains

Sitting by my window, on a hill in the Himalayas, I look out to a sea of mountain ranges. Like soldiers they march into the distance in the gathering light of a new day. The morning is young, and I can hear the mountain crows caw in their rough, majestic voices. Other bird-sounds, thin whistles and delicate chirrups, rise up in the intervals when the crows pause.

I am now over eighty years old. A very grand

age, when I am allowed to sit back and listen to birds, examine the shapes of mountain ranges, and let my mind wander. These days I find my thoughts going back to my childhood all the time. And that is the period I now write about in my books, as in this one. We become like little children when we are old!

I have lived in the Himalayas for most of my life, but my first memories are not of the mountains, but of the sea. When I think back and search for the earliest scenes from my life, I remember the sea: a vast field of water, and sunny white sails of dhows and smaller boats billowing in the wind. I also remember a forest of nodding flowers and patches of red, yellow, green and blue light on a wall. And I remember a little boy who ate a lot of kofta curry and was used to having his way—in other words, a spoilt brat!

These are images from my early childhood in a seaside town called Jamnagar, which is now in the state of Gujarat. But there were days that went before all this, days of which I don't remember anything. It was when I was only an infant and the first memories were yet to be formed. But I am a writer, and what is a writer without an imagination? So let me start at the very beginning.

~

I was born a very long time ago—in 1934, in Kasauli, which is in the hills of Himachal Pradesh. It's a pretty little place even now, and I imagine it must have been even more picturesque so many years ago. My mother had a sister who lived there and it was to her that my mother went when I was to be born. My mother's parents lived in Dehradun at the time, not too far from Kasauli, so it is surprising that she did not go to be with them. But the lives of grown-ups are full of many secrets and surprises. I'm sure there was a good reason for choosing Kasauli to bring me into the world.

I was named Owen Ruskin Bond by my father. 'Owen' means 'warrior' in Welsh. I wonder what my father had imagined about his infant son's future character, but I never did get anywhere close to becoming a warrior! So it is a good thing that the name Owen has been forgotten and I have been just Ruskin ever since.

A month after I was born, my mother and I came to Dehradun to be with my grandparents. My father had taken up a teaching job in Jamnagar, and we would be joining him some months later. Meanwhile, it was in Dehradun, or Dehra as it was simply called, where I spent the first few months of my life. What would it have been like, I wonder. I think there were plenty of walks in prams in the pleasant late summer months of the Himalayan foothills. I can imagine my mother and aunts taking turns to push the pram down the tree-lined streets as they walked to the cafes and shops in the centre of the town. Here there were cinemas and clubs and little shops selling aaloo tikkis and chaat, ice cream and pastries (none of which I would have got to eat at the time, but I made up for that in good measure some years later). There were photo studios too, and my picture was taken by a photographer in one of these. That photo of a fat baby me was sent to my father by my mother and I still have it in my collection.

Life in Dehradun must have been made more exciting by my Uncle Ken. He was my mother's brother and an eccentric man who had strange ideas for entertainment. Here is an Uncle Ken story from my infancy that could well have happened.

My mother, tired and with a headache from the sleepless nights that a new baby brings with it, had gone to take a nap, leaving my uncle in charge of me. He was not the most reliable of babysitters (or reliable about anything, for that matter) but there was no one else around, and my mother was desperate for a few hours of unbroken sleep. I had been fed, bathed, changed and I should have been happy and sleepy. But babies don't follow the normal laws of nature or households. They are ticking bombs that go off according to their own internal baby logic. And so it was that I set up a fuss and a bother soon after I was left alone with Uncle Ken.

'Now, now, hush Ruskin,' my uncle murmured absentmindedly as the first notes of protest emerged from the bundle inside the cot. His words usually had no effect on anyone—from my grandmother to the various girls he tried to woo—and it wasn't likely they would make baby Ruskin change his mind about setting up a mighty wail. The small unhappy snuffling soon became a full-throated howl. Panicked, for he had promised he would try to do at least this much for my mother without making a mess, Uncle Ken looked around urgently for a solution. The rattle? The little tin drum? The wind-up toy that made a clanging sound? He tried one after the other but they just made everything worse, and Uncle Ken was sure he was the one getting a headache now. My face was red with anger, and I was getting ready for a long session of complaints.

'Oh no, oh no,' Uncle Ken went into quiet hysterics. And that's when the brilliant idea came to him. Within minutes he set it into motion. There was no way he was going to be called a good for nothing. In fact, if anything, he was going to be called a babysitting genius. So it was. My mother arose a good three hours later, rested and happy. She wondered how poor Ken had managed all this while. She should make some tea for him, she thought. To her surprise, the nursery room was empty, as was Uncle Ken's room. Slightly worried, she now went out to the garden, thinking he was walking me there. But no, there was no sign of nephew and uncle here either. 'Surely, he has not gone off to the bazaar with the baby,' she muttered to herself, puzzled. And then she spotted us, out of the corner of her eye, under the big neem tree at the other end of the garden.

Uncle Ken had put that old lullaby with the lines 'Rock a bye baby on the treetop, when the wind blows the cradle will rock' to work. He had rigged up an outdoor cradle for me. An old bedsheet had been turned into a makeshift hammock that looped over a low branch of the tree. In the crook of the sheet I had been laid along with all my blankets. Uncle Ken sat under the tree with a string tied at one end to the cradle and at the other end to his big toe. As he sat there, reading the cricket news in the paper, he swung his leg gently and the string moved the cradle back and forth.

Did I look happy? Yes, indeed! Over my head

was the mighty green canopy of the neem. Birds flew in and out, some looking quizzically at this new nest-like creation under the tree. As the cradle rocked gently, the sky swung in and out of the branches. Green and blue, blue and green. Do babies recognize colours? Perhaps I did and perhaps I liked what I saw. Or maybe it was the plump squirrel which sat there peering at me that amused me. Instead of roars of protest, soft gurgling sounds came from the cradle.

'Ken!' my mother shouted. 'Surely you couldn't have done this!'

'Indeed I did,' Uncle Ken was jolted out of his reading and surprised and not a little hurt at the tone of my mother's voice.

'You put him in a bedsheet and hung it from a *tree*? What if the sheet had torn? What if he had fallen? What if...'

Uncle Ken raised a commanding hand. 'None of those things happened. We are fine.

The baby is fine. I am fine. And did you know, England will surely lose the Ashes this time...'

Uncle Ken looked on in surprise as my mother snatched me up and marched off indoors. There really is no way to understand the workings of a mother's mind, he decided, lighting up his pipe in relief and untying the string from his toe. Now he could sleep in peace under the tree.

So the months at Dehradun passed. My grandfather had built a house here in 1900 and had lived in it with his family since 1905. The house, made of the smooth, rounded stones from the nearby riverbed, was a compact and comfortable place. There was a garden with fruit trees, a neem and a banyan, and flower beds that my rather stern grandmother had planted and guarded over.

My grandfather himself was more fun-loving. He would disguise himself as a vegetable vendor or a juggler and wander around in the bazaars. One day he fooled even Granny; she had bought tomatoes and onions and was haggling over the price of turnips before she realized the man selling her the vegetables was her husband. He was also in the habit of bringing home unusual pets—owls, frogs, chameleons and, on one occasion, a hyena, which chewed up the boots in the house and had to be released back into the forest very quickly.

But I never got to know my Dehra grandfather, for he died the year I was born. Many years later, I brought him to life in my stories. Some were stories I had heard from my mother and aunts, some I made up. I also made up stories about my Dehra Granny (making her less forbidding!) and uncles and aunts. They all feel very real now—like an alternative family. I am glad they feel like family to many of my young readers too.

~ 2 ~

Beware of the Lion!

Soon our time at Dehra was over and it was time for my mother and me to join my father in Jamnagar. Jamnagar or Navanagar was a little port town in the Kathiawar peninsula on the west coast of India. Steamers plying across the Gulf of Kutch stopped there, as did large Arab dhows, which made a lovely sight with their great white sails. This part of the country was full of small, independent states that were not a part of British India.

My father had taken a job as a teacher with the Nawab of Jamnagar. He started a small palace school for the little prince and young princesses there. This is where I spent the first six years of my life.

My first real memories are of life in Jamnagar. I remember so many things from those days—the rich yellow of Polson's Butter; colourful tins of J.B. Mangharam's biscuits with cherubs and scenes from Indian mythology painted on them; drives in our maroon and black Hillman convertible; and postage stamps from the Solomon Islands—smoking volcanoes and cockatoos with big showy crests.

We had a beautiful gramophone, a black, square box-like wonder, which was probably the first love of my life. It was one of those wind-up affairs, and you had to change the needle from time to time. The turntable took only one 78 rpm record, so you couldn't just relax and listen to an uninterrupted programme of music. You were kept busy all the time—changing records, changing needles and constantly winding the machine vigorously so that it wouldn't fade away in the middle of a song. But I loved putting the records on the turntable and then setting the needle carefully down as the music wafted out.

It is strange that now music comes from mobile phones and everyone everywhere is walking around with little earplugs that pump the sound right into their ears. Just the other day a pretty lady was walking down the road towards me, nodding and bobbing her head and pouting her lips. I was feeling very flattered for having kindled the fire of romance in her even at my age, but then she passed me without so much as a glance and I heard tinny dance music issuing from her headphones. My ears burned with the insult! (I got even with her that night by dreaming of her walking into a large goat and being chased all the way down to Landour bazaar. The goat ate up her fancy mobile and headphones.)

But I am digressing. Let me return to Jamnagar. My parents had quite a collection of records, and among those was a selection of nursery rhymes put to music, bought especially for me. One of them began: 'Oh, what have you got for dinner, Mrs Bond?' I delighted in listening to this one in particular, because, of course, our name was part of the song. But also because it mentioned dinner—and I was a chubby child, happy to eat whatever was offered to me.

The dinner (and all other meals) came out of the kitchen, from the pots and pans and karhais and degchis under the command of the khansama, or cook. His name was Osman, and he took care of all our meals. I was a fan of Osman's, because he made the best mutton kofta curry in the world, and told me some very tall tales. Osman and Ayah were my first friends and storytellers. Had Osman put as much spice in his curries as he did in his stories, we would have been a household on fire.

In the afternoons, when I was usually alone—even Ayah would be outside, talking to my sister's nanny, or taking a nap—I would join Osman in the kitchen as he boiled or chopped or cleaned the meats and vegetables he would later cook for dinner.

A typical story session would go something like this:

'You see this goat I am going to cook, baba? He reminds me of the great lion of Junagadh.'

'Where's Junagadh?'

'Two days by foot from this very house, but you can get there in your motor-gaadi in five-six hours. I worked for the Nawab of Junagadh, who took me along when he went hunting, with ten elephants, twenty dogs and a shikar party of fifty-sixty men—he was a very rich nawab, he would get himself weighed in diamonds on his birthday and give them away to his begums... But I was telling you about the great lion. It needed two full-grown goats or one bull every day. It only ate male animals. And when it could not find goats or bulls, it hunted men. Women were safe.'

'Did the lion come to hunt you?'

'No. But it took my masalchi.'

'What's a masalchi?'

'The boy who helped me prepare the meats and vegetables and washed all the dishes. We were part of the hunting party and sharing a small tent. When I saw the boy was gone, I beat my chest and cried all day, till all my tears had dried up. After that I had to sleep alone the rest of the time we were in the camp. I lit a big fire outside my tent to keep the lion away—someone had told me lions are afraid of fire.'

'Did it stay away, then?'

'No, baba. Lions are not afraid of fire at all. The beast returned and walked around the fire and stuck its head in through the flap of the tent. I was still in mourning for my poor masalchi, and when I saw the lion which had eaten him up, I was very angry. I picked up the big iron tawa on which I was making rotis and hit the beast on its nose. The tawa was hotter than the fires of jahannum, and that son of Satan—'

'What's jahannum?'

'It is where bad people go after they die and are roasted in big tandoors. Little boys who keep interrupting a story go there too.'

'Sorry.'

'So I struck the lion's nose with my tawa and it let out a roar and fell backwards into the fire burning at the entrance, let out another roar, and fled into the jungle. We heard the beast roaring in agony all night!'

'Did the nawab give you a reward?

'No, baba. He was a rich badshah, but not a generous one. Not like our Jam Sahib...'

I did not need to ask who this Jam Sahib was. He was the Nawab of Jamnagar. Jam Sahib's kingdom was orderly and life here was good for us. It was here, in the houses we lived in, the gardens I played in and the walks I went on with Ayah that my first memories were formed. Osman was the first storyteller in my life. He would tell me about

man-eating tigers and dangerous crocodiles, ghosts that haunted the highest tops of trees and chudails—female ghosts with their feet turned backwards—who came floating down to earth to search out naughty children. He had a way of adding masala to anything that happened around us. Events from his past always sounded mysterious and exciting, and I could not wait to hear more and more stories from him. I gobbled his tall tales the same way I gobbled cakes and laddoos and kofta curry. So much that each time I eat mutton kofta curry even today, I think of Osman driving away the lion by brandishing his hot tawa!

~ 3 ~

Aeroplanes, Laddoos and Orange Pips in My Stomach

The Tiger Moth rose, higher and higher into the brilliant blue sky. What is a Tiger Moth, you ask? It is a small airplane that was built first in the 1930s. These somewhat flimsy planes had four wings, two seats, and from where I sat inside one, it made a lot of noise! The planes were popular with the Royal Air Force as well as with civilians and those who wanted to learn how to fly. At Jamnagar there was an aerodrome, where some young royals would fly these planes over the surrounding countryside. The Tiger Moths were the most popular aircraft for this, though why anyone would ever want to sit in one and watch the solid earth fall away rapidly, was something my four-year-old brain could not comprehend.

My mother had brought me to the aerodrome to watch the planes take off and land. It was a beautiful day and for a little boy, the thrill of watching would have been just fine. Till one of the young pilots spotted us. He had met my mother at some dinner party earlier, and was anxious to keep up a good impression. He ran over to us, a big smile on his face.

'Mrs Bond, how lovely to see you. What brings you here today?'

My mother smiled and replied she was there to show me the planes. The man now noticed me, holding my mother's hand tightly and the idea mushroomed in his head.

'Come up in the plane for a spin, Mrs Bond,' he grinned.

My mother was an adventurous person, and I am sure she would have been tempted. But what about me? The man was ready with his solution. I could come up in the plane too! I looked up anxiously at my mother. Surely she was not going to get into one of those machines? Her eyes were shining and she held my hand a bit more tightly. Yes, we were going up in it.

Before I knew what was happening, I was squeezed into the cockpit of the plane and the propeller fans were whirring at great speed, setting up quite a racket. As I sat up straight and looked ahead, the plane started taxiing, and then with a little hop it rose away from the ground. My stomach seemed to fall away and I dived for my mother's lap. The plane rose higher and I thought fondly of the

earth below me. 'Look up, Ruskin,' my mother coaxed, her mouth close to my ear.

I opened one eye and then the other. Far away below us was the green of the earth. I could clearly see the fields, ready for cultivation. Where there were no fields there was brown earth. Dotted among the open fields and uncultivated land were some streams flowing gently like thin blue ribbons. Suddenly, the pilot shouted, 'Watch out!' and while we grabbed each other, he put the plane into a low swoop. We flew over the heads of startled sheep and goats and their herders. One little boy, I still remember, crouched low down, then as we roared away he jumped up and waved at us. I was holding on too hard for dear life to wave back.

We lurched and bounced in the sky and then suddenly, below us, were the waves of the Gulf of Kutch. Blue water, white waves, billowing sails of the ships and boats going up and down the gulf. A few wisps of clouds and birds wheeling around. Then the nose of the plane turned up and we rose up steeply. This was too much. I yelled in horror hoping for some god somewhere to stop this flight of fear. The plane levelled up and when I opened my eyes we were flying over a cricket field. Tiny men in whites were running up and down. I

wished I was there among them rather than hanging from the sky like this.

My prayer was answered shortly, and the enthusiastic pilot landed back on the airstrip with everyone in one piece. I walked off the plane with shuddering knees and a distinctly queasy stomach. I would hate flying for the rest of my life!

~

The cricket that I saw from up in the air was a regular feature of life in Jamnagar. Jamnagar was the home of Indian cricket. A previous ruler, Ranjit Singhji, had played Test cricket for England. Promising young players like Vinoo Mankad were learning their cricket in Jamnagar. My father was no cricketer, but we would attend most of the cricket matches which involved visiting teams from England or elsewhere. I was taken along to these games too. Everyone who mattered would be there—the Jam Sahib (in immaculate sherwanis and churidar pyjamas, when he wasn't on the field himself) and his retinue, his family members and his European and Indian staff, visiting officials, neighbouring princes—and refreshments were constantly being passed around by bearers in smart white turbans.

I don't remember much of the cricket—I was too small to appreciate a batsman's technique or a bowler's guile—but I do remember the men in white, the thump of the ball being hit, and the players running around as they scored runs or stopped the runs on the field. I also remember the refreshments offered freely at the cricket matches.

'Don't eat too much,' warned my mother, as I helped myself to gulab jamuns, jalebis, rasgullas and laddoos, all washed down with fizzy lemonade—those being the days before cola drinks came to India. But of course I always ate too much, and I would be sick when we got home. There, I was handed over to my ayah for further scoldings: 'Too many laddoos, too many laddoos, how much baba eats!' and she nicknamed me 'Laddoo' which gradually became 'Ladla' or Sweetheart.

I did not mind being Ayah's Sweetheart. She was a very *comfortable* sort of woman, large and loving, and at the age of four or five I could appreciate her pillow-like structure, soft and smelling of spices, and my mother's eau-de-cologne.

She was probably from one of the fishing communities of Kathiawar or from the poorer Muslim families from the north of India who worked in Christian and Anglo-Indian households. She must have been in her thirties and was unusually large and broad-limbed for an Indian woman, and shaped like a papaya. I was told she had a family of her own but I never saw them, and she never spoke of them. She was the one I spent the most time with at home—she stayed all day, washing my clothes, giving me a bath and telling me stories about jinns and fairies and the snake that transformed into a handsome prince by the loving touch of a beautiful princess.

Ayah had large, rough hands. She could use those hands very effectively to deliver a few resounding slaps, because I really was a little devil. But her anger vanished as quickly as it came when she saw me break into tears. And then she would break down herself, and cover me with big, wet kisses and gather me into herself.

Eau-de-cologne was the scent of the day, there being nothing else in the shops except something called 'Evening in Paris' which (as I learnt later) was distilled in Aligarh and bottled in Bombay. In the depths of the bazaar you could also pick up little bottles of local perfume—heady stuff, distilled from roses or jasmine, guaranteed to linger on the user for weeks.

Ayah fancied a little eau-de-cologne from time to time, and I would smuggle the bottle out to her. After sprinkling it over herself, the bottle would be quietly returned to my mother's dressing table. Ayah loved me for this little service. 'A friend for the sake of advantage,' as Aristotle put it!

Came the day when my mother couldn't help noticing the very low level of perfume in the bottle.

'Who's been using my eau-de-cologne?' demanded mother bear.

'I used it on the dog,' I said quickly, already a good dissembler. 'She was smelling horribly.'

Poor Beauty, our aging Alsatian, did smell a bit but not too badly. However, she was given a good bath in a Dettol solution, and sulked for weeks, not being fond of bathing.

Left alone with Ayah one day, I tried to teach her to dance the waltz, but she simply

collapsed in hysterics on the veranda steps, squealing with laughter.

'Get up, get up,' I said. 'Get up and dance with me.' But she refused and wouldn't stop laughing, and annoyed, I called her 'Ayah-papaya' and then ran like a rabbit.

Later, I put her into a rhyme, which must have been my first literary effort. It went something like this:

Gobble-gobble said the turkey,
Honk-honk said the goose.
Cluck-cluck said the little hen,
Squeak-squeak said the mouse.
Clang-clang went our motor-car,
Bang-bang went the wedding band.
Katar-katar went the porcupine,
Tootle-tootle went the train.
Nothing-nothing said the goldfish,
And the earthworm said the same.
Sleep tight, says Ayah-papaya,
And God protect my little baba.

Notice that most of my rhyming occurred at the beginning rather than at the end of my lines. Already, I was finding it more fun to do things in reverse. It's a useful skill to have, especially when life begins to get difficult and boring.

Ayah taught me many things. One of these was the eating of paan. I didn't care for the taste—somewhat bitter, because of the betel nut and lime—but I was fascinated by the red juice, which Ayah would spit with great accuracy in different corners of the overgrown garden. When my parents were out, she would make me a miniature paan—I think she added a little sugar in it—and I would chew the paan and sit in the kitchen, gossiping with her and the cook. Before my parents came home, Ayah would rinse my mouth with warm water, and with her rough fingers she would scrub my teeth clean.

If I swallowed an orange seed, Ayah would

say an orange tree would grow inside me. Being an imaginative child, this rather worried me because orange trees, I was told, had thorns on them. I did not want to worry my parents unduly, so I took my problem to Mr Jenkins, who lived next door. He heard me out seriously, thought about it for a few moments, then said: 'Don't worry, it will only be a small tree.' Still worried, I consulted Osman, who laughed and said, 'Your ayah is just a gapori, don't listen to her.'

'What's a gapori?' I asked.

'One who makes up stories—and exaggerates. Go and tell her you've swallowed a bean.'

I did, and she said, 'Oh, baba, now you'll have a bean-stalk growing inside you!'

'And there will be a giant living in it?' I asked.

She burst into laughter, seeing I'd caught her out.

'Osman says you're a gapori,' I told her. And she and Osman had a terrible fight. She chased him around the house and forgave him only when he said he meant she was a pari, a fairy, not a gapori.

Still, I think I learnt something about telling stories from Ayah, as I did from Osman, although I had no idea that I would become a gapori of sorts one day.

~ 4 ~

Walks with Daddy

My father—I called him Daddy—was a quiet, scholarly sort of man. Yet, in his company I would find my greatest joys and adventures from the time I was a small baby. He was taken from me when I was only about ten years old, so we did not have much time together. But my childhood is bathed in memories of him and all that we did together.

One early memory is of how I would get into the bath with him. My own baths took place in a large tin tub. I liked splashing around and flooding the bathroom, and my mother preferred to keep a distance, leaving poor Ayah to take the soaking. Sometimes my father joined me and we would sing sea-shanties together. Shanties were sailors' songs, sung in unison while they were at work on the old sailing ships. My favourite was 'What shall we do with the drunken sailor?' And whenever this question was sung out by my father, I'd sing back: 'Put him in a tub and wet him all over!'

These tub-baths with my father became something of a tradition, and continued for several years. He called them 'rucktions'. I don't find this word in the dictionary, so I presume he invented it. 'Creating rucktions!' He enjoyed it as much as I did. Perhaps it took him back to his own childhood. On these occasions he would be quite boyish and noisy. He was 'Daddy' to me. That was what I always called him. Not 'Father' or 'Dad' or 'Papa'. My mother was 'Mum' or 'Mummy', but my father was always 'Daddy'.

Among my father's many hobbies was photography, and I still have the pictures he took with his Rolleicord camera of the infant Ruskin a few hours old, a day old, two days old, a month old, etc.

His other passion was stamp collecting. His collection of stamps was his great pride and he preferred staying at home with it rather than going to parties and official dinners. And a wonderful collection it was, with postage stamps from all over the world, neatly arranged in special albums—an album each for India, Britain, Australia, Ceylon, Zanzibar, and various island nations in the Pacific. Some were recent stamps, others rare issues from the past, and Daddy went about completing sets and mounting them in the handsome albums. Registered letters would arrive from

the famous firm of Stanley Gibbons, enclosing samples or purchased items, and the Gibbons stamp catalogues would occupy pride of place on the bookshelf.

Often, of an evening, I would help my father sort through cigar boxes full of loose stamps, while in the background the Italian opera star Gigli would be singing one of his famous arias. Whenever the record finished, I would rush to the gramophone to change the needle and the record.

The Jamnagar sea-front was only a twenty-minute drive from our bungalow, and some evenings we visited the little port called Rosi Bundar, which had a retired British naval officer, Mr Bourne, as port commander. My small hand in my father's, we strolled up and down the pier, and I explored with him the harbour and beach, bringing back seashells and cowries of great variety. It was on these walks that I got to know the taste of salty sea air, the screaming of the seabirds and the white waves on the blue waters. I would skip around my father, sometimes holding his hand, sometimes running ahead. If he stopped to talk to anyone, I would quietly start digging around on the sand or look for pebbles of various interesting shapes. There really is a lot at the seaside to keep a young child busy!

On one occasion, I brought home a small crab, which lived in a spare bathtub for several days. Osman kept asking if he could cook it, but I wouldn't let him. I was very attached to the crab—for two or three days, I think, and then I forgot all about it. Finally, Ayah took pity on the poor creature and dropped it into a nearby well.

A small British steamer was often in port at Rosi Bundar, and my father and I would visit the captain, a good-natured Welshman who gave me chocolates—a great treat in those days, for Jamnagar was too small a place for

Western confectionary shops. I was ready to go to sea with the captain, convinced that chocolates were only to be found on tramp steamers!

One day, Daddy took me for a trip in an Arab dhow. These dhows or sailing boats dotted the sea around the port, their large sails billowing in the wind. Some say these were first made by the Arabs, while others claim it was the Indians who came up with boats of this design. Mostly slender, the boats came in many sizes, and were used to transport all kinds of goods up and down the west coast. They sailed all over the Indian Ocean with crews of just a few men, or even up to a thirty, on the bigger dhows.

The boat on which Daddy took me was a big one. He had got talking to the captain, one day, while we were out walking on the seaside, and the captain had taken a liking to this man with his sandy haired boy and had invited us for a short trip. I was so excited the morning of the boat ride that I was ready to run out of the house as soon as I woke up, without changing or brushing or even thinking about breakfast—a most unusual thing for me, for till date I rarely forget about food. But Ayah would have none of it. She caught hold of me and made me get dressed in a smart pair of shorts and a loose cotton shirt. She then fondly combed down my unruly hair, made me wear my shoes and by the time I was ready to be presented to the world, Osman had placed the breakfast of toast, marmalade and eggs on the table.

'And where is baba off to today?' he asked no one in particular, looking somewhere between Ayah and me.

Since my mouth was full of toast, Ayah replied, telling him about the boat ride.

'Ah baba needs to be careful. The sea is full of dangerous creatures. Big fish, small fish,

fish that will eat up men before they allow the men to catch them...'

My eyes grew round as saucers even as my mouth continued to work on the toast, bits of crumbs flying out.

'Fish that eat men?' I sputtered.

'Yes, baba. Never take your eyes off the water and never turn your back to the sea. These fish sometimes also have human faces with mouth filled with sharp teeth. The teeth are like daggers. They will catch you by the waist of your pants and pull and pull. Baba, if you feel anyone pulling you, remember to jump away—even if your pants tear. You must never look at them in the eye, though. Some of them change their forms into beautiful maidens, and then you are completely done for. You will never return from the sea. If you survive, you will spend the rest of your days on a lonely island with these fish-men. We will never see you again.'

By now my breakfast was almost swallowed whole and I was on the verge of choking on my milk. As I placed my glass down with a thump, considering the possibility of having to live on a lonely island, Ayah had had enough.

'Osman, go back to the kitchen and finish your work. Stop scaring baba like this!' she shouted at him. 'Fish-men indeed! Who has ever heard of such nonsense?' She turned to me and wiped my milky mouth that was hanging open. 'Don't worry, baba. Don't listen to this man. You go tell Daddy that you are ready to leave now.'

I quickly climbed down from the chair and went in search of Daddy, who was waiting for me. Holding his hand tightly I looked back once at the house as we turned the corner. What if I was really caught by a big fish and carried away into the depths of the ocean? Would I ever see this house again? What about my mother and my little sister? And what about dear Ayah?

Would she cry for me? Would she run up and down the seashore calling out to her darling Laddoo? And my father? Who would look after Daddy if I was away? There would be no one who could arrange his stamps, to run and bring his cigar boxes, clean his camera, put the correct records in the gramophone. Without realizing it, I sniffed largely and sadly. Daddy looked down at me in surprise. I was rarely quiet when we walked together like this, yet today I seemed almost heartbroken, thinking of my imaginary impending loss to the world.

'Are you all right, Ruskin?'

'Yes, Daddy. I will keep an eye out for the fish-men. Nothing will happen, don't worry.'

'Fish...men? Did you mean fishermen? They are not dangerous at all, you can watch some of them laying their nets if you want,' Daddy was quite puzzled now.

'No, Osman said...' and my story was lost in a tumble of words that I don't think my father fully understood. But it did not matter because we had reached the place where the dhow was docked.

I forgot all about fish with fearsome glinting teeth as I looked up at the boat that was waiting for us. It was quite large, and the white sails were flapping in the wind. Many men were rushing around loading sacks, while others were checking the sails and shouting out to each other in some unknown tongue. The whole place was bursting with activity and while there was running and shoving here and there, it also all looked quite well planned and that everyone knew what they were doing.

The captain walked up to us and shook my father's hand. He was a dark, tall man from the Middle East and he ruffled my hair as he grinned down at me. His hands were rough and hard, I remember. I was dying to ask him about the possibility of being kidnapped by large fish, but I don't think anyone would have heard me above the din. Some uneven planks were laid out and we balanced on those to get to the dhow. Many helpful hands stretched out to help me and I hopped down on to the boat smartly. There was a strong smell of fish in the air and I wanted to hold my nose badly, but that would have been rude. Instead, I trailed after my father as he talked to the men, examining the sacks and watching the sails being made ready. In a few minutes the sails filled with air and we set off into the sea. Our destination, I learnt now, was a port that lay a few miles south of Jamnagar. The dhow was transporting fruits from one to the other.

As the boat picked up speed once we were on the open waters, I realized there was something worse than Osman's fish-men. It was the movement of the boat on the waves that were making it rock worse than a cradle being pulled by crazy mermaids. Up and down we lurched and the water splashed and slopped into the boat. The wind pulled hard and the boat raced away on it. I clutched on to Daddy's hand afraid of being swept into the sea where strange fish and mythical creatures waited to devour me. Daddy patted me on the head and didn't object at all to his hand being held for two hours in a tight grip. I remembered Osman's warning and tried not to turn my back to the water. But it was not always possible to do that when we were being thrown and lurched around by the unruly waves. I felt myself going a bit green as my breakfast threatened to tumble out of my mouth. Only the shame of appearing a baby in front of these swarthy sailors made me hold it all in.

Whenever I could I took a peek at the waters. There was no sign of any fish. But till today I remember the sun glinting blindingly on the waters. There were streams of silver

all around, molten and beautiful. Above, the sun was a ball of lava and the heat bathed us, making our clothes stick to the skin. But then a huge spray of water would rise up and slap us on our faces. Other than the voices of the men, there was a strange silence everywhere, as though we were the last people on earth, heading to an unknown destination.

Of course, much of this is what I think of the whole journey now. As a child of four or five, I was perhaps only thinking of when we could be back on land. In my mind I even yearned for a fish-man or two to jump out of the water and provide some welcome diversion—as long as it was not me who was carried away for their lunch!

We sailed down the coast for a couple of hours before being put ashore at one of the smaller ports. I must say I was never happier to see land. Daddy and I sat in a Jeep that was headed to Jamnagar and we reached home in time for a late lunch. Thankfully, Osman was resting after his morning toils by then, and had nothing more to add to his tall tales of the morning. And as for me, I was glad to be back on terra firma, in the safe cocoon of home and bed. I have always liked having my feet set firmly on the ground ever since.

~ 5 ~

The Room of Many Colours

We lived in at least three homes in Jamnagar in all the years we were there. First there was a rambling old mansion whose roof leaked every time it rained. After this—or maybe before—a wing of the old palace, which looked like a ruin from the outside but was cool and comfortable inside (though we had to share it with bats and bandicoots). Finally, we moved to the 'Tennis Bungalow', a converted sports complex, which was bright and airy and where we stayed the longest.

Jamnagar was where my habit of walking really began, because it was full of spacious palaces, lawns and gardens. By the time I was four, I was exploring much of this territory on my own. Although I was afraid of aeroplanes and sailing-ships, I was not troubled by birds, beasts or reptiles. The old walls around the palace grounds were infested with snakes of various descriptions, and I saw them often enough on the lawns or the driveway. Envious of their swift, gliding movements, I tried crawling about on my belly at home but I wasn't much good at it. Curious though I was, I knew instinctively that if I did not bother them or get in their way, the snakes would keep away and allow me to pass. They did not send me into a panic, as they did Ayah, who would scream 'Saanp, saanp!' and dash into the house, urging my father or the cook to come out and vanquish the reptile. The snakes seldom entered the house, as they had to climb a flight of steps in order to do so, and most snakes prefer not to exert themselves unduly. Unless, of course, there's a frog or a fat rat in the offing, and then they can move with great speed in order to snap up their breakfast or dinner.

My father's schoolroom and the Tennis Bungalow were located in the grounds of the old palace, which was largely uninhabited, and full of turrets, stairways and mysterious dark passages that I loved to explore. One afternoon, I slipped out while everyone was in deep slumber. I was in the mood for adventure, and to lie next to Ayah as she dozed in the heat was not my idea of fun. I also knew she would wake if I made the least noise, so I tiptoed out barefoot and stopped to put on my slippers only once I was safely outside. The garden was also in deep sleep. In the afternoon haze the trees were still, the branches waiting for even a tiny gust of wind to stir them back to life. An old disused well was the home of countless pigeons, their soft cooing by day contrasting with the shrill cries of the brain-fever bird at night. 'How very hot it's getting!' the bird seemed to say. And then, in a rising crescendo, 'We feel it! We FEEL it! WE FEEL IT!'

Marigolds and cosmos grew rampant in the tall grass between shady trees. I loved walking among the white, light purple and magenta cosmos flowers, always friendly, nodding to me, inviting me closer. Unlike the roses, which seemed very snobbish to me, perhaps because their thorns prevented me from getting close.

I slipped into the disused part of the palace through a door that hung lopsided. No one bothered much to come here, and no one imagined there would be anything of any interest here. But adults usually don't think of the curiosity of children when they decide what is important and what is not. Place an empty shell of a palace right under a child's nose and expect him to never walk around and examine all the nooks and corners? Only those who have forgotten their own childhoods would do such a thing. The sloping roof, the turrets, the dark and winding staircases of the palace had been beckoning to me for many days now. I did not know what I was going to find inside, but it was eerie and shadowy and my mind was already running away with thoughts of hidden treasure, runaway bandits, and ghostly spectres walking the corridors. 'Brave boy apprehends bandit hiding in abandoned palace'. I imagined the next day's newsreader announcing on the radio. I squared my shoulders, pulled myself taller and plunged in through the half-broken door.

Sadly, there was not even a whiff of any

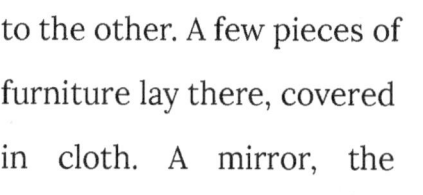

treasure or lawbreaker anywhere. There were rooms, dusty and silent. My slippered feet pattered around as I went from one to the other. A few pieces of furniture lay there, covered in cloth. A mirror, the glass brown with age, hung from a wall and I stood in front of that for a while, making funny faces. The glass had also become a bit distorted and from some angles my face appeared either too long or too wide. I swayed from side to side, imagining myself on the dhow and watched as my reflected face went from looking like a squashed pot to a long pole with eyes placed on top.

The staircases were winding and steep and I climbed right to the top of the main tower that afternoon. There was only one large room at the top. It was circular and it ran right around the tower. Perhaps it had been a place for nawabs and their wives to sit and look out into the distance once. But now, when I entered the room, I drew in my breath in surprise. The room had glass windows going right round it, and each square pane was stained with a different colour. Red, green, pink, orange, the sun's rays fell through these panes and the room floated in a sea of white light. It was

the most magical thing I had ever seen—even more magical than the silver sea from the boat.

This room became my favourite place for days. I would climb up to look through different panes of glass at a red or yellow or rose-pink or indigo or parrot-green world. It was nice to be able to decide for oneself what colour the world should be!

Look at the sky one day through red glasses and see for yourself how the clouds look strange and enchanted in their pinkish hue. The crows are dark brown spots and the trees in the distance are bathed in a red light. The room was always empty, and it stayed in my memory as a lonely and charmed place.

Some forty years later, I wrote a story about an ageing princess who had lost her mind and shut herself up in this room after she'd been prevented from marrying the palace gardener. I called it 'The Room of Many Colours'. But at that time, there was no princess or even a gardener from the looks of the palace garden. There was only a little boy called Ruskin, imagining what it would be like to live in a green-coloured world.

~

As the reader may have guessed by now, at Jamnagar there were very few children for me to play with, except when the little prince sought me out, which was rare, or when the royal children had birthday parties. But there was always Ayah to fuss over me, Osman to tell me improbable stories, and my father to take me for walks, so that, for several years to come, I was to feel more at ease with adults than with other children.

A place I enjoyed visiting was the state farm that lay just beyond the palace grounds. It had ducks and geese, hens and roosters (which tried valiantly to wake me up at dawn with their loud crowing but failed). My favourite birds were the turkeys, bred mainly for Christmas and New Year banquets, for it was only the Europeans in the state who really appreciated turkey meat. 'Gobble, gobble, gobble!' went the turkeys whenever I passed them. I liked their colourful plumage and naked wattled heads. They were always waiting to be fed. The ducks and geese roamed all over the place but the turkeys had a pen to themselves, as did the pigs—pink, plump, imported all the way from England.

A middle-aged Welsh couple, Mr and Mrs Jenkins, ran the farm for His Highness the Jam Sahib. I don't think they had any children, and they seemed quite happy spending time with each other and the birds and animals, with books and magazines providing some variety. There would be stacks of *Punch*, *Country Life* and *Picture Post* lying about on their veranda. My reading skills were still rather limited, but I liked going through them for their pictures and cartoons.

I possessed only two books during those Jamnagar years—a big book of nursery rhymes, and a battered edition of *Alice in Wonderland*. It was by reading *Alice* (with help from my father) that I learnt to read, and my favourite characters were the Mad Hatter, the March Hare, the Dormouse, poor Bill the Lizard, the Cheshire cat, and the philosophical caterpillar smoking his hookah. I could not really identify with Alice, who seemed a superior sort of person.

All this reading happened outside the classroom, because I wasn't enrolled in a school. Sometimes, when I felt like it, after wandering around the gardens and the old palace corridors, I would put in an appearance at my father's classes. Among the pupils were the four Jamnagar princesses—Manha, Jhanak, Ratna and Hathi. All of them had short hair and were really beautiful. I, however, for quite a while did not know that they were girls. They would be dressed in trousers and jackets and I thought they were boys I could talk to. I got a shock when my father told me one day that they were girls! For some days I was overcome with shyness and refused to go to the schoolroom.

But the temptation to play with Hathi, the youngest and the closest to me in age, proved stronger. So one day, I got over my shyness and peeped into the room. My father had set them some tasks and the girls were deep in thought and their work. Daddy saw me sidle into the room and only smiled a little smile. Manha and Jhanak were too engrossed in their sums to look up. Hathi saw me and gave me a bright, welcoming smile. She sat up straight and pointed to a chair next to her. Relieved that no one was laughing at me for thinking of them as boys, I trotted up to her. It had been some days since I had been able to practice my newfound trick—reading a page upside down!

So as Hathi bent to her work again, I stood in front of her and read her essay on the page upside down. Little did I know then that this habit will remain with me to this day! Even now, when I find a book boring or difficult to read, I turn it upside down and read it like that. Everything seems much more interesting that way. If I had ever wanted to be a detective, I think this may have helped me. Alas, that is something I have never been, although I do read lots of detective books!

The princesses had one brother, the little prince, who was the heir to the throne. But he was not yet in school. Sometimes he would come over to the bungalow to play with me. The sweet-natured son of the Jam Sahib's secretary was another playmate. And there was my sister Ellen, two years younger to me, whom I would push around the garden on a tricycle. What did we all play? I think hard, but I can only guess it was something noisy and active. All of us had a lot of energy to burn, and I am sure tearing around the garden in a game of football would have been perfect.

I think back to those days and try to remember the faces. I know them from the pages of the album, in the photographs my father took of us. In the album, the pictures are browned with age. In my mind, I see them through many-coloured glasses, sometimes green and sometimes red. That is the magic of childhood.

Wars and Mad Kings

World War II broke out when we were into our third or fourth year in Jamnagar, and the end of the war was not in sight, though of course we were insulated from it. I don't remember hearing much about the war at home. It was many years later that I learnt of the horrors in Europe and East Asia, and also of the Jam Sahib's contribution to the Allied war effort through a remarkable act of humanity. As Poland was invaded by German forces, he opened his doors to refugees from that helpless country. Several hundred children and women who had fled Poland in small ships that travelled from port to port and were denied entry by the authorities everywhere—including the British governor of Bombay—were brought to Rosi Bundar by the Jam Sahib. He put them up in a special camp in Balachadi, close to his summer palace, where they stayed till the end of the war.

The Jam Sahib was one of the few enlightened rulers in pre-Independent India. One of his neighbours, the eccentric Nawab of Junagadh, fled to Pakistan, taking with him scores of his favourite dogs—he'd kept a few hundred, but had to leave most behind. Fortunately the lions of the Junagadh forests were not affected by political upheavals, and today represent the only lions in existence on the Asian continent.

The Maharaja of Alwar, in Rajasthan, was another unusual ruler of that era. He kept a menagerie of beasts and would drive them all into an amphitheatre to see what they would do to each other. According to my mother, who lived very briefly in Alwar with Daddy, this maharaja modelled himself on the Roman emperor Nero, and took a sadistic delight in watching various animals tear each other to pieces—a tiger mauling a buffalo, a bear wrestling with a python, a young leopard being crushed by an elephant. These and other tales of the Indian Nero were passed on to me many years later.

Strange things happened in some of India's princely states in those far-off days. But not in Jamnagar.

The world may have been in upheaval then, but my own memories are of an almost idyllic time. When I would go out to roam in the garden, the cosmos flowers were always happy to see me, nodding happily in the breeze. But a somewhat proprietorial koel would keep wanting to know who I was. Koo-who, it would call. Koo-whoo? Koo-whoo? Sometimes at night I would sit on the veranda steps, reluctant to go any further into the darkness, but after a while I began to enjoy the buzzing and rustling sounds in the garden, and the soft hooting of the owls.

And there was of course that wonderful gramophone at home and its box of records. I could always turn to it when I felt lonely or bored, or when my parents' frequent quarrels made me unhappy. Wind up the machine, change the needle, place the record on the turntable—and the room would be filled with the wonderful voice of Chaliapin singing 'The Song of the Volga Boatmen'; or Gigli singing 'Santa Lucia'; or dear old Gracie Fields singing 'Over the Garden Wall'. There were about fifty records in the box, and I'd played them all hundreds of times; they became real friends and companions.

So that when my father said he'd joined the Royal Air Force and that we'd be leaving Jamnagar, the first thing I asked was, 'Daddy, will we be taking the gramophone with us?'

'Let's see,' he said. 'We can always get another one.'

'No, I want this one,' I insisted. 'We can't leave it behind.'

And so it was agreed that the gramophone would come with us.

'And what about Ayah?' I asked 'Will she come too?'

'You're too big for an ayah now,' he said. 'And while I'm away you'll be in Dehradun with your mother and Granny—you won't be needing an ayah. And besides, your ayah's home is here in Jamnagar. She has a husband and grown-up children. She can't leave them all behind.'

'Well, can't she bring them too?'

'Your Granny's house isn't big enough for so many people. And sometimes your cousins will be staying there too.' The cousins he referred to were the children of my mother's four older sisters, my aunts Beryl, Enid, Emily and Gwen—the former two from my grandfather's first wife. So far I hadn't seen any of them.

What did I take with me when we left Jamnagar? The gramophone, of course, although this (fortunately for me, as it turned out) was to stay with my father in Delhi. A couple of books, including the battered old copy of *Alice*. And a pile of comics.

Unlike most Indian railway stations, the Jamnagar station was a small one, minus the milling crowds. We had a coupé to ourselves. We settled in comfortably, and as my parents checked that all our bits and pieces of luggage had been stowed away, I quickly took a window seat. The train windows did not have glass like they do these days. Neither was there any question of air conditioning. If you pulled them up, the windows stayed up, kept in place by some hinges, and one could poke the head out and watch the world go by.

As soon as I looked out, I found Ayah in front of me on the platform, her eyes and face wet with tears. Osman had bade me goodbye at the house, when we left for the station and had stopped himself from telling a railway monster story or two. But Ayah, my real mother, she of the soft skin and rough hands, she who scolded and loved and fed and bathed me, she who loved me like one of her own children, came with us to the station and shed copious tears. 'Baba,' she smiled sadly. I held out my hands and she took them for the last time in her warm, rough ones. That last touch of my first love.

But Ayah could not stand in peace for too long. The platform was filled with vendors selling all kinds of food items and they were busy trying to push those in through the window. There was tea and there were piping hot pakoras and cool, refreshing lemonades. But as interesting as these food items offered to us were, I was warned not to eat any of the mouth-watering concoctions. Only a month previously a family friend had got on to the train in Calcutta, hale and hearty, and two days later his corpse had been carried out of the compartment upon its arrival in Delhi. Cholera could take you away within twelve hours. The food served at the station restaurants was usually safe, but somewhat bland and uninteresting. Instead, we were carrying with us plenty of chicken and turkey sandwiches, a large basket of fruit (courtesy the palace) and a

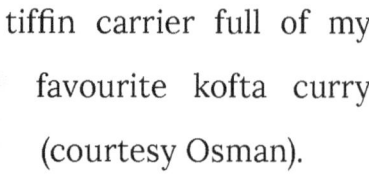

tiffin carrier full of my favourite kofta curry (courtesy Osman).

Soon, too soon, the guard's whistle blew, the steam engine gave a snort, and the train moved slowly out of the station. I leaned out, waving goodbye to Ayah. She grew smaller and smaller and as the train picked up speed, she was gone. I sat back on my seat, still too young to know that some goodbyes are forever. I would never see Jamnagar or Ayah again.

As my mother got busy trying to soothe and settle in my little sister who was fussing in the unknown environment of the train, my father and I got into a deep discussion about trains, types of engines, speed and railway engineering. Neither of us knew much about the subject, but it was fascinating to listen to the click-clack of the wheels, the occasional hoot of the horn, the whoosh of the steam escaping overhead, and to wonder what it was like to live in the villages and towns and cities we were passing through.

It took almost three days to travel by train from Jamnagar to Dehradun. In those days, India was perhaps the best place to undertake a train journey—for train travel at its best is all about romance; about the boundless outdoors, where anything can happen. Look out of the train window into the vast open fields, and the true size of our country comes alive. There are streams and canals and rivers and fields. Men and women working in their farms, sweeping their yards and looking up as the train rushes past. Sometimes one can wave out to a lonely cowherd standing by the rail track, and watch as the sun goes down on yet another day in the lives of the people of this great country.

The trains were not as crowded then as they are today, and provided no one got sick, a long journey was something of an extended picnic, with halts at quaint little stations, railway meals in abundance brought by waiters in smart uniforms, an ever-changing landscape, bridges over mighty rivers and khuds, forests and farmlands, everything sun-drenched. The air was crisp and unpolluted—and we let it rush in—except when dust storms swept across the vast plains. Bottled drinks were a rarity, the occasional lemonade or 'Vimto' being the only aerated drink. We made our own orange juice or lime juice and took it with us.

Passengers thrown in together for the duration of a journey would politely chat with one another. Or not so politely—and this has not changed in all the years I have travelled by train. On many train journeys, I have been quizzed on everything about myself—who am I, where did I grow up, am I married, what do I do for a living, when did I come to India and how come I speak English like an Indian... On hearing that I am a writer many have been very puzzled—they wonder why I haven't found myself a decent job—while others have been appreciative and have asked the names of books that I have written. It is only recently that some people have begun to recognize my name and remember the name of a book or two of mine that they might have read. Once, a co-passenger who had refused to look up from his copy of the Sherlock Holmes adventure *A Study in Scarlet*, while everyone around him carried on about where they were going and where they lived, finally put down the book and looked at me sternly when I said I was a writer. He was as suspicious of me as he would have been if I had said I was the prime minister of the country, or a famous spy.

'And what books have you written?' he asked me.

I named one or two.

'Never heard of them,' he announced, and retired behind his novel in a satisfied manner.

Crestfallen, I ate a soggy railway sandwich, till a girl came up to me with a copy of a book by Enid Blyton for me to sign. I took out my pen and signed with a flourish: 'I hope you enjoy this book as much as tea and scones and clotted cream! Love, Enid.'

The girl looked very happy to have got her book signed by Aunt Enid.

But all this was much, much in the future. The time I sat on the train with my parents and sister and all our belongings and left Jamnagar, I was just about six years old. I was leaving behind all that I had known and recognized of the wider world until then. The sea and the dhows, the palace with the overgrown garden, the room of many-coloured windows, the cricket matches, the afternoons spent walking on the beach with my father—all these were gone, never to come back.

As we approached Dehradun that winter of 1940–41, I woke up early one morning and looked out of the open window at dense forests of sal and sheesham (I learnt the names much later); and here and there a little forest glade or a stream of clear water—quite different from the muddied waters of the wide streams and rivers we had crossed the previous day. As we passed over a largish river—my father told me it was the Song River—we saw a herd of elephants bathing. And as I turned my head to look at the gentle giants till they were out of sight, we entered the Doon valley, where fields of flowering mustard stretched away to the foothills.

The train creaked to a halt at Dehradun station. It is still a small station, and at the time it was tinier still. For three days we had let the soot and dust of the plains of India come in through the open windows, and now when we got off the plain we were black as coal miners. My mother had run a wet cloth over our faces to make us look a little presentable. Holding my father's hand, I hopped off the train. It was winter and the air in Dehradun was crisp and nippy. A whiff of eucalyptus hung in the air, mixed in with the station smells. Coolies rushed up to us to help us take our luggage to the tonga. Even today, getting off a train means haggling with and choosing a coolie among the many who descend on us. In some ways I think the scenes at Indian Railway platforms have not changed at all! Daddy haggled with them, but not too much, and by the time we walked out of the station, Dehra's bracing winter climate had already revived us.

We took a tonga and creaked and clip-clopped pleasantly along quiet roads. Scarlet poinsettia leaves and trailing bougainvillea adorned the garden walls, and in the compounds grew mango, litchi, guava, papaya and lemon trees that Daddy pointed out to me throughout our tonga ride. The tonga driver deposited us at the gate of my maternal grandparents' home. As the gate swung open, I saw the neem tree where Uncle Ken had made me rock-a-bye-baby once. I wondered what life in Dehradun would be like.

~ 7 ~

The Wrestlers

'Crazy! Come, boy.'

From up high, I watched my grandmother's grey head appear and then disappear as she called out to her dog. Crazy was a chocolate-coloured dog of mixed breed who had made the house his home for some years. He was usually to be found curled up fast asleep by the gate, which he pretended to guard. This usually meant a short woof and an eye that opened to lazily take in the person who was about to enter. Everyone other than the postman was welcome. For the postman, Crazy reserved his most ferocious barking and capering around. Once the postman went away, Crazy would flop down at his spot, exhausted from all the work he had done for the day.

Crazy and I had become good friends quickly after we moved into Granny's house. My father left soon after to do his training and then posting with the Royal Air Force (RAF), so I now needed to make a new friend. There was no Ayah here, nor an Osman. There was no palace to explore either, but there was Granny's garden with its tall trees, neat beds of flowers, the well-kept lawn, and Crazy to play hide and seek with.

Today, I had decided to play a trick on Crazy and was hiding in a tree. It was a bit unfair that Crazy had the advantage of being able to smell out the person who was hiding.

But here, far up in the tree, among the broad leaves on a high branch, I was well hidden with a good view of all that was going on below me.

It was an old banyan tree behind the house. Its large, spreading branches hung to the ground and took root again, and they were covered with thick green leaves. I was very well concealed, and I came here often and sat propped up against the bole of the tree to read a comic or watch the world below, on the road outside the compound wall: an English sahib in a sun helmet. A memsahib holding a colourful sun-umbrella. A lady in a sari with a basket of papayas balanced on her head. A man with a little hand-drum, and a monkey dressed in a red frilled dress and a baby's bonnet sitting on his shoulder.

I also watched Granny as she searched for Crazy. My sister cycled about in the lawn on her tricycle. My mother and Aunt Enid sat in the garden, chatting. Uncle Ken, who was in Dehra between visiting his various cousins and married sisters, had wobbled off, whistling, on his cycle, perhaps to the bazaar. It was quiet and peaceful up here with my eyes nearly closed, but I had to be careful to not fall off. I wished I had thought of bringing up a snack with me. I was now at an age when I was always hungry and a slice of cake or a cheese sandwich would have been just right.

I flicked away a red ant that was marching up to me, ready to investigate and report to its headquarters. A squirrel that had stopped its chirping when I appeared on the branch was now used to me, and had started its high-pitched chirp all over again. Its tail bobbed up and down and its quick black eyes darted around, looking for fruits and berries and other delectable squirrel food. As I watched it, the squirrel froze for a few seconds. I followed its gaze, and was startled by a giant yellow beak poised above my head. I backed away onto the closest branch, fearing an attack. I recognized the bird from my father's postage stamps, where it was strange but small, and a resident of faraway Botswana or Kenya. I hadn't expected to run into it on a friendly banyan tree in Dehra! But the hornbill, relaxing in a great hole in the tree trunk, did not move and looked at me in a rather bored manner, drowsily opening and shutting its eyes. After some time, I lost my fear. I was certainly too chunky to be hornbill food, and anyway it was only interested in smaller bugs and insects. For several moments, we all sat in silence looking at each other—the squirrel, the hornbill and I. The tree was our home—safe, stocked with food (for them, not for me, unless I decided to snack on a caterpillar or two), leafy and comfortable.

The moment of peace was shattered by Crazy setting up an awful racket below. The squirrel squeaked and ran for cover. The hornbill flapped its wings and flew off. And I nearly fell off the tree in surprise. The postman had come on his rounds and Crazy had found him simply by falling asleep near the gate. I descended from the tree to calm Crazy down and we romped around in the garden, chasing each other like hyperactive schoolboys.

That evening, Granny mentioned the words I had been dreading for a long time. 'It's time Ruskin started going to school.' Mother, Granny and everyone else had a long discussion. I think I was quite forgotten about. But as a result of this, I soon found myself in a small convent school at Hampton Court in Mussoorie, the Convent of Jesus and Mary. My mother came to drop me off, and I kicked and screamed and made a terrible scene but quietened down when I realized my tantrum wasn't going to make her change her mind.

I hated that school from the first day. And I

was still hating it a year and a half later, when I left. I was lonely, a misfit, unused to the company of hordes of shouting, screaming boys and girls, all of whom seemed unhappy.

My boredom and restlessness at school were relieved by the arrival of colourful picture postcards from my father, who never failed to write to me. He would send me cards from Lawson Wood's 'Gran'pop' series, featuring an ape who attended cocktail parties, went up in hot-air balloons and danced in the rain. Together with these postcards came messages from Daddy that there were books and toys waiting for me when I came home.

At the convent school, I finally made friends with a boy named Buster Jones, who disliked the place as much as I did. Together we made plans to run away, and to that end we began saving up biscuits, slices of bread, rusks and other edibles that could sustain us on our flight to freedom. These bits and pieces were hoarded away in our lockers, but were soon discovered, and as punishment we were made to stand all day outside Reverend Mother's office. But we continued to make plans for our escape, although neither of us had any idea where we would go.

But my escape did come about, although in an unexpected way. My father was now posted in Delhi, and he decided to send for me to spend some months with him. The truth dawned on me later—that my parents had decided they could no longer remain husband and wife. My mother had decided to keep my infant brother, born only the previous year; my sister would be sent to our paternal grandmother in Calcutta; and I would go to Daddy. But even had I known the truth then, I'm not sure I would have been unhappy. I was a child and wouldn't have understood that the situation was serious, or that it was permanent. I would only have been glad to be leaving the dreary school and its joyless, disciplinarian nuns. My mother drove me to Dehradun station, from where I would take the train alone. I was not to feel anxious or afraid, she said, there were some friends travelling by the same train who would look out for me. I wasn't at all anxious at the thought of travelling alone to Delhi. In fact, nothing could have made me happier; I was going to be with Daddy. I sat happily in the compartment of the train and it was soon chugging its way to Delhi. There I would be met by Daddy at the station, and though I didn't know it then, the most joyful year of my childhood would unfold.

~

World War II was at its peak now. Almost all of Britain's resources were being used for the war, and India's mood for independence was growing stronger every day. It was becoming clear that the British would have to leave and the Raj would finally come to an end—but when it would really happen was anyone's guess. Meanwhile, the British were everywhere in Delhi, as their largest colony got pulled deeper and deeper into the war that was raging far away. Men, materials, food—everything that could be shipped away—was being sent to Europe. The Indian leaders had once supported the war effort during the previous World War, some twenty-five years ago. Who would have thought another world war would break out so soon? This time, the leaders of the Indian struggle for independence were not willing to be as supportive. Mahatma Gandhi and his followers were keeping up the pressure on the British to extract more political reforms, more space for Indian voices in the way the country was ruled, and soon it would all culminate in the call for the British to Quit India.

When I first went to Delhi, we lived in a little two-room brick hutment in the wilderness near Humayun's Tomb. There was an entire line of them, built some distance from one another and separated by trimmed hedges; temporary and very functional abodes designed for serving officers and their families. The area is now a busy and sought-after part of Delhi, but in 1942 it was a scrub jungle where blackbuck and nilgai roamed freely.

Daddy went to work at nine and came back around six. On Sundays, and sometimes Saturdays, he was free. His office was in the Air Headquarters in South Block which was attached to a wing of the Viceroy's palatial residence, which later became Rashtrapati Bhawan. His work in Codes and Cyphers was very secretive and mysterious, and if he broke any important enemy codes, he didn't tell me.

In winter he wore his navy-blue RAF uniform; in summer, khaki. He always looked dapper and smart—he was a good-looking man, short and spry, with a boyish charm. I envied that uniform, and often posed in his caps and braided hats, and insisted on being photographed in them. And what's a uniform without salutes? I saw my father's juniors salute him and I saw him salute his senior officers and soon I was clicking my heels and saluting everyone in sight!

Daddy was always up early, making our breakfast, beating up the cream to make my favourite white butter. After breakfast he would be off, and I'd be left to my own devices for the rest of the day. There were some comics to read and a large postcard collection to go through. And there was the old gramophone, and the old records—I don't think my father had time to buy any new ones. But I did not mind; the gramophone was a great companion, filling the room with the glorious sounds of operatic arias and duets. Daddy had told me to be careful with the records and store them flat, otherwise they could assume weird shapes in the heat and become unplayable.

That first summer in Delhi is etched clearly in my memory. I had never been in so hot a place, and I remember those scorching winds of June—the loo, the 'evil' dust-laden wind from the deserts of Baluchistan and Rajasthan which is now rarely experienced in Delhi. But it took me only a few days to get used to the heat. The bhisti, or water-carrier, came around ten or eleven, delivering fresh water from his goat-skin bag. There were no taps in the hut, so he filled the tub and a large drum and splashed water on the khus, a reed matting that hung across the front door. This had a wonderful cooling effect, which didn't last more than half an hour, but I loved the tender, refreshing fragrance of the khus and the smell of damp earth outside, where the water had spilt. It would be many years before air conditioning came to Delhi. We had a small table-fan in the hutment, but as yet no electricity.

The cool of the rooms attracted various creatures, and I had to look out for scorpions and centipedes, which sometimes took shelter in shoes or empty mugs or the clothes' basket. One morning I opened the lid of the gramophone to find a large scorpion asleep on the turn table. I yelled for help, but there was no one around. So I shut the gramophone lid with a bang, and did not open it until my father got back in the evening. By that time the scorpion had mysteriously disappeared.

There were geckos, wall lizards, which sometimes fell on the table or on the floor with a soft thwack. At night, numerous jackals set up an endless series of wails, but they did not venture into the houses; unlike the wild cats, who came at any time of day or night, foraging for food. Sometimes they hissed and growled at me, but cats did not frighten me and I hissed and growled right back!

Despite all this wildlife in and around the hutment, I was quite happy to be on my own, a king of the castle, confident that my father would be home at six, ready to talk to me or take me out or bring out his stamp collection. Albums and boxes of stamps would be spread out on the dining-table, and by the light of a kerosene lamp we would discuss new issues, or the rarity of old ones, often referring to the prized Stanley Gibbons catalogue to see if a set was complete.

On Sundays we went on walks or little excursions in and around Delhi. Humayun's Tomb was close by; a handsome edifice that rose gracefully above the surrounding wilderness of babul and keekar trees, a testament to human enterprise, even if it had served as the burial place for many kings, queens and princes. The Purana Qila, or Old

Fort, was not too far away either. Here my father showed me the steps to the library and observatory that was a favourite haunt of Emperor Humayun.

'He'd been waiting to see Venus the evening he died,' he told me.

'How did he die?' I asked.

'They say he was going down the steps in a hurry and he tripped and fell to his death. He fractured his skull.'

It was an eerie, winding staircase, dark and forbidding. I could well imagine someone tumbling down those steps.

Sometimes we went further afield, to the Red Fort and its pavilions overlooking the sluggish but as yet unpolluted river.

'If there be a paradise on earth,

It is this, it is this.'

So said the inscription on the wall of one of the Mughal emperors' pavilions. Being tired and hungry after trudging around the ramparts of this massive citadel, I did not find it paradise enough, and was only too happy to retreat to the refreshment rooms at the Old Delhi railway station. Here we felt quite at home with Uncle Fred, the station superintendent, one of my father's few friends.

The refreshment rooms were on an upper floor of the station, free from the din of the railway platforms, the shunting of engines, the whistle of the guards, the shouts of the coolies and that cacophony of sound which was (and still is) a feature of large Indian railway stations. The food was limited fare but nevertheless acceptable to a 'growing boy'—chicken or mutton cutlets (Railway Cutlets, they were called), a mutton or vegetable curry, pilau or rice, and a flavourless blancmange or custard pudding. I ate the cutlets and curry, but left the pudding. Refrigeration was in its early days, and ice creams were a rarity.

Back home, we kept our drinking water cool in a surahi, an earthen vessel which was kept in a shady spot. There was also a dolie, a small cupboard with a wire-mesh front, in which fruit, vegetables and kitchen supplies could be stored. The legs of the dolie were kept in saucers of water to prevent ants from getting in. Even so, some of them managed to get across to feast on their favourite foods—sugar cubes, bananas, cream rolls—anything sweet and sticky. You could keep out snakes, rats, lizards and bats, but you couldn't do much about the ants. They were constantly on the march, heading resolutely in the direction of their objective. They were like a German Panzer regiment: disciplined, unwavering.

After a few months, we gave up the hutment. It had been meant for family use, and I was the only indication of a family. Daddy's superiors were always wanting to know why my mother wasn't around to look after me. So he rented rooms on Atul Grove Road, a quiet cul-de-sac off Curzon Road (now Kasturba Gandhi Marg), very close to Connaught Place, which was then the commercial and professional hub of New Delhi.

On one side of the road were half-a-dozen bungalows occupied by officials of the telegraph department, and my father had taken the rooms on rent from one of the residents. On the other side of the road stood the offices of the department, flanked by the humbler quarters of the lower rungs of the department's employees—peons, cleaners, chowkidars and their families—and there was an open ground, well-grassed, in front of the building where the children would play in the evenings.

Among them was Joseph, the son of one of the resident officials—a dark, skinny boy from southern India, well-mannered, smiling, eager to be friends. We met quite casually. There was a letter-box, one of those red pillar-boxes, at the end of the road, and I came out of the house to post a couple of letters for my father. A boy of about my age also crossed the road to post a letter, and thrust his hand into the opening at the same time as I did. We had to hold hands in order to facilitate a smooth release.

'Pleased to meet you,' said the boy. 'I'm Joseph.'

'I'm Ruskin.'

'Which school do you go to?'

'I don't go to school,' I said.

'Lucky chap!'

It was the beginning of a gentle friendship that lasted through the long summer of 1942 and the winter that followed.

After six in the evening it was possible to run around a little, play football on the open ground, have a wrestling-match with Joseph. Wrestling with Joseph was always great fun. As the sun slowly disappeared, in the orange light two boys wrestled on the playground. This was not a fight that had to be settled with fists and blows. It was a proper wrestling match with rules and points. One of the boys was dark and quite slender. The other, fair, plump and brown-haired. The boys had forgotten everything else around them—the heat, the dust rising in plumes as their bodies thumped and fell, the voices shouting encouragement from the periphery of the ground. The fair-haired boy was obviously stronger and was winning. Over and over again he managed to pin the other one down as they rolled and caught one another in vice-like grips.

'Joseph Joseph Joseph!' shouted one group of cheerleaders.

'Go Ruskin!' yelled a few scattered voices, perhaps more out of pity.

As I held down my friend Joseph and won the wrestling bout, the crowd broke into scattered applause. Being much heavier than him, I generally got the upper hand, but he would never give up—he would wriggle out from under me and lock me in some intricate arm or leg hold, and I would have to use all my superior weight to break free and sit on top of him. The children from the department's quarters would watch these bouts with great interest, cheering whenever Joseph got the better of me—for, being fair-skinned and the son of a British officer, I was identified with the colonial oppressors—but no one interfered; they knew instinctively that we were two friends engaged in a trial of skill and strength.

That summer and then the winter passed swiftly and happily. I went for walks with

Daddy all over Connaught Place. We went to bookstores for the latest comics, to music stores for records, to Kwality's and Keventers for ice creams and milk-shakes—Daddy spoilt me thoroughly!

We also went to Delhi's famous cinema halls—Regal and Plaza and Odeon—which were quite grand back then—high ceilings and carpets on the floor and a single massive screen on which magic happened. In that year I must have seen some forty films with Daddy—from early Disney classics like *Bambi* to fantasies like *Thief of Baghdad*. Comedies were my favourites—the madcap adventures of Laurel and Hardy and the Marx Brothers.

I became quite the cinema addict. And I started to read some more—comics and magazines and anything else I could get. If left to myself, I would have never emerged from this cocoon of happy days spent with Daddy. I had him all to myself and he had all the time for me. We were friends—to have a parent who is also your best friend is one of the great joys of life, especially when you are very young.

But rarely do such things last, and for us, too, the enchanted time came to a close when Daddy fell ill a few times in quick succession. It was recurring malaria. He had to go to the hospital each time, and the fever and the infection left him weak and shivering for days. Then one time, Daddy returned from hospital looking wan and tired. And he had news for me.

'I've found a good school for you in Shimla,' he said. 'You'll like it there.'

'But I like it here,' I protested. 'Why do you want to send me away to school again? I can read and write. You've taught me how to do sums.'

'But I can't teach you Physics and Chemistry. Besides, another hot summer in Delhi won't be good for you. You've lost your pink cheeks and your eyes look yellow.'

'So do yours.'

'In my case it's due to the quinine I have to take. But seriously, it's high time you went to school again. Everyone says I spoil you. You've had over a year's holiday!'

'Another year won't make any difference. If you like, I can go to school in Delhi, along with Joseph.'

'The problem is, I may be transferred soon. This war is going on for longer than anyone thought. I may be sent to Karachi or Calcutta, or even North Africa.'

'Why can't I come with you?' I asked.

'I won't be allowed to keep you with me, son. I'll have to share digs with other officers. In Delhi, I can make my own arrangements, but not when I'm sent to other postings.'

And so it came about that I was to resume my interrupted school career.

Daddy took a fortnight's leave, Uncle Fred put us on the night train to Kalka, and we were off to Shimla, the summer capital of India.

It had all happened very suddenly, and I didn't even get a chance to say goodbye to Joseph.

But I haven't forgotten him. Some friends—their eyes, their touch, their words—cannot be erased from our memory.

~ 8 ~

The Tunnel of Friendship

I was inside an egg. An egg made of cardboard, and painted in a rather careless manner with slaps of white and yellow, and I had been made to squeeze myself into it. I cannot say I was feeling too pleased about it, but then very rarely in school does one get to do as one exactly pleases.

The band struck up a tune, and the singers started chanting the familiar rhyme: Humpty Dumpty sat on a wall... I was pushed up, egg and all, to a cardboard wall and made to perch there. Two eyeholes had been cut into the eggshell so I could see where I was. I listened to the words carefully. There was my cue: Humpty Dumpty had a great fall... And off I fell from the wall. The cardboard was supposed to shatter on the impact of the fall, creating a spectacular scene of cracking egg and rolling Humpty. But alas. The best laid plans of Miss Khanna, our drama teacher, had come to nothing. The cardboard refused to show even a crack, and I rolled around, bouncing slightly, safely enveloped in the eggshell. Needless to say, all the king's horses and all the king's men got their hands on unbroken Humpty quite easily and did a good job of pretending to put him together. Meanwhile, I could hear the school auditorium resounding with the laughter of about a hundred children. It was one of my more successful stage outings.

I was now in the prep school of Bishop

Cotton School in Chhota Shimla. This was where my father had brought me some months back and the headmaster had agreed to take me in though it was the middle of the term. The headmaster was an unremarkable sort of man, usually too busy with his violin—which he played, in my opinion, quite badly. The school, though, was a great improvement on the horrid convent in Mussoorie and the boys had a fairly good time in the classes and the fields. The teachers were sometimes strict but never unreasonably so.

Even though I had been out of a classroom for over a year, I found that I was not too far behind the others in my studies. All that time I had spent with my father and the stamp collection had made me knowledgeable about places. And because I would also get to listen to so much of grown-up talk, I had a good idea about politics and world events of the time. My grammar and composition were good and my skill at numbers passable. So while I had not been too happy to see my father leave—he was the only person in the world I really ever wanted to be with—I soon settled down in boarding school.

They were a rowdy but a friendly lot at prep school, and I had more fun there than I did at senior school later on. We were quite a scruffy lot. We fought, we played in the dust, made a lot of noise, made friendships, got into trouble, played pranks on the teachers and had spectacular pillow wars that resulted in a storm of cotton and feathers in the dormitories.

The exploits of comic-book and sports heroes thrilled us more than anything else. The Biggles books, featuring the daredevil pilot James Bigglesworth, were a rage in those years, and when word went round that my father was in the RAF, the boys began to look at me with new respect! I made the most of it and asked Daddy to wear his smart uniform when he came up from Delhi to see me.

'Does he fly bombers?' the boys would ask me.

'All the time.' I'd lie and make up stories about his heroic exploits in the skies!

But I had competition. Young Abbot claimed that his father, a one-time hunter before he turned animal-lover, raised tigers and bears for zoos around the world. Abbot had grown up playing with tiger cubs and he showed us scars and scratch marks on his back and thighs to prove it. We believed him and were in awe of him.

I remember other boys from prep school. Bimal Mirchandani had the skinniest legs in the school and was called 'Bambi', after the little gazelle in the Disney film. (He became a good wrestler when he was older! Which just goes to show how wrong we are to judge people only by their appearance.) Kellnar was taking a course in body-building, even at that young age, but was defeated by the fact that he had a very long neck and splayed feet; we called him Donald Duck. Mehta Junior was a sleepwalker, and he caused a sensation once by sleepwalking off the dormitory roof and falling into the headmaster's flower bed without any damage to himself.

Some of the boys were working on complicated literary works. One of my classmates (I forget his name) was writing a novel—a detective story—on toilet paper. Due to the wartime paper shortage, he was using those little thin sheets that came in flat packets instead of rolls. In any case, we were not allowed toilet rolls because the boys frequently used them to make streamers across the dormitory or in the corridors.

I had not, as yet, taken up writing—that was still two or three years distant—but my interest in acting and cinema prompted me to produce a one-act drama, inspired by the film *The Brighton Strangler*, which was running at the Shimla Rivoli. The script was simple. I played a demented serial-killer; all I had to do was strangle several victims (played by my class fellows), who would scream, choke, gurgle or beg for mercy as they perished at my hands. Alfred Hitchcock would have approved. But Mr Priestley, the prep school head, did not, and I was reprimanded and told to use my talents for something more wholesome.

Days at the school passed swiftly, though not quickly enough for me, for I knew once the winter holidays came around I would get to be with my father in Delhi. And so it was. I spent a happy time in the city with him, doing everything we loved to do together, and I was back in school again, this time happier and more confident.

~

The journey up to the school in Shimla was made by train. The bigger trains from Delhi, Ambala and elsewhere terminated at Kalka, just below Shimla. Here, all the boys would be put into one compartment in the small hill train that chugged up the mountains. Kalka Station was tiny and the sudden influx of so many boys would transform it into a noisy, unruly place. That is, until our teachers showed up. There would usually be one teacher on the train accompanying the students. We would hope it would be someone who would allow us to sit where we pleased and let us open up our packed food whenever we wanted. Mr Oliver was usually the one given this task, and though he was not unfairly strict, he wasn't too friendly with us either. He preferred to read a book through the journey between the times he walked up and down the compartment to make sure no one was doing anything silly like poking their heads out of the windows or planning to pull the chain that would bring the train to a halt.

There would be plenty of shared food and chatter and laughter on the train. Put twenty boys of various ages together, and hear how loud it can get! Once, on this journey, the hills were still covered with snow. It had been an unusually harsh winter and there had been snow above Kalka. The train groaned and whistled and puffed through the 100-odd tunnels that dotted this pretty route. Usually the hillsides were full of rhododendron trees in bloom, the red flowers like little flames lining the way. But this time, everything was bare. There were patches of snow all over and brown trees wherever we looked. The train, which went slowly at the best of times, travelled even more slowly, the driver hooting the horn often. Finally, as evening fell and we were still some miles from Shimla, the train came to a halt. What happened? Everyone stood up and craned their heads out. Mr Oliver marched off towards the engine. He came back after a short while and said that the driver had decided that it was too risky to take the train on the snowy tracks in the dark. We would have to spend the night in the train.

It was an unbelievable adventure! A night on a stationary train in the pitch dark and silence of the mountains. When the noise of the boys died down, I heard something I had not known earlier—a deep and bottomless silence. We all took out our warmest clothes and wore them, huddled together in the small compartment. Mr Oliver gathered all the food we had with us and, by torchlight, distributed it among us equally and as fairly as possible. I still remember what I ate for dinner that night—poori sabzi, bread and jam and a boiled egg! The night passed with us trying to sleep on our seats, our heads falling on to each other's laps and shoulders. It was a friendly, cosy sort of night, though none too comfortable, but then young boys and girls can sleep just about anywhere if they are tired enough.

In the morning we woke up to a wondrous sight. It had snowed lightly, and all around was a thin sheet of white. The sun was trying to come out, but it was a weak sunshine. The cold bit into our noses and ears. Finally, it was decided that it was still too risky for the train to move on the tracks. We were out of food and water, so we would walk the last few miles into Shimla. Our luggage stayed on the train, to be collected from the station later. We all clambered out and, in a strict line that Mr Oliver made us stay in, we made our way through two tunnels and a few miles of frozen land to finally reach Shimla. We were cold and hungry, but it had been the best school-going adventure for me ever.

~

In this way, the first few school terms passed, and I got more and more used to living in a boarding school. When my father got some leave, he came up to meet me. Once, we had planned to spend the day walking up to Jakhoo Hill with some pastries. Unfortunately, it started raining, and so we spent most of the time in a café. I did not mind, as my father was there with me and the café menu was extensive. We talked, and my father told me of his plans to move with me to England once the war was over. I was not too keen on this. India was the only place I had ever known as home. But independence was round the corner now, and my father would be out of a job once the air force men were demobilized. That rain-filled, misty day in the café, drinking hot chocolate and sampling the shammi kababs and cakes is etched into my mind forever—it was to be the last time I ever saw Daddy.

He was posted to Calcutta, Karachi and

elsewhere, and I could not join him for the next holidays. And then, one day, my whole world came crashing down. Mr Murtough, one of the masters, called me out to the grounds, made me sit on a bench and told me that my father was no more. His illness had finally caught up, leaving him weak and vulnerable to other infections, and he had passed away in Calcutta. I was about ten years old, and I had known love and the safety of a parent's shelter only from my father. Without him, I was as good as an orphan. I had not seen my mother in two years. I mourned for a long time for this gentle, quiet man who had shown me what living decently while following your heart means. I think I have mourned him ever since and have never stopped missing him.

~

Yet the world carries on, as if nothing has changed. Individual sorrows are swept aside in the daily march of events. School and holidays and terms and exams continued, and I went through the paces. In some time I was out of the prep school and in the senior school that was located on another mountain side in Shimla. Things were not as easygoing here as in the prep school. But there were a few masters who were kind and understanding and I began to read more and more in the library now. Classics like *Treasure Island* and *Kidnapped*, the works of mystery and crime writers like Arthur Conan Doyle, Agatha Christie, the entire works of P.G. Wodehouse, and my favourite among all of these—Charles Dickens. I read these books, indeed devoured them, when I was not on the football field, where I was part of the school playing team.

My friends in senior school included Azhar Khan, who came from Lahore; Cyrus Satralkar, from Bombay; and Brian Adams, an Anglo-Indian boy from New Delhi. We called ourselves 'The Four Feathers', the feathers—of a falcon, a peacock, a parakeet and a woodpecker—signifying that we were companions in adventure, comrades-in-arms. Our occasional escapades were confined to breaking bounds when opportunity arose, or sharing our food parcels, or going into town together on Sunday afternoons to watch movies. Satralkar received the largest number of food parcels from home, and he became the most valued member of the group.

But it was Azhar who became my closest friend. He was a quiet, intelligent boy, the ideal companion on long walks or scrambles down the hillsides. While I was losing much of my shyness, and was not as much of a loner as before, he was an introvert and took no part in the clowning around that boys tend to do.

Even before we began talking to each other, Azhar and I developed an understanding of sorts, and we'd nod to each other when we met in the classroom corridors or in the dining hall. We were not in the same house. The house system practiced its own form of apartheid, whereby a member of, say, Curzon House was not expected to fraternize with someone belonging to Rivaz or Lefroy. But these barriers vanished when Azhar and I found ourselves selected for the school hockey team—Azhar as a full-back, I as goalkeeper. A good understanding is needed between goalkeeper and full-back, and we were on the same wavelength. I anticipated his moves, he was familiar with mine.

It wasn't until we were away from the confines of school, classroom and dining hall that our friendship flourished. The hockey team travelled to Sanawar, on the next mountain range, where we were to play a couple of matches against our traditional rivals, the Lawrence School, which was then still a military school (my father's old school, in fact). Azhar and I were thrown together a good deal during the visit to Sanawar, and in our more leisurely moments, strolling undisturbed around a school where we were guests and not pupils, we exchanged life histories. Azhar was from the North-West Frontier Province, and he had lost his father, too—he was shot in some family dispute. A wealthy uncle was seeing to his education, as the RAF was seeing to mine.

I had already started writing my first book. It was called *Nine Months*, but had nothing to do with a pregnancy; it referred merely to the length of the school term, the beginning of March to the end of November, and it detailed my friendships and escapades at school and lampooned a few of our teachers. I had filled three slim exercise books with this premature literary project, and I allowed Azhar to go through them. He was my first reader and critic. 'They're very interesting. But you'll get into trouble if someone finds them,' was his verdict.

We returned to Shimla, having won our matches against Sanawar, and were school heroes for a couple of days. And then my housemaster discovered my literary opus and took it away and read it. I was given six of the best with a Malacca cane, and my manuscript was torn up. Azhar knew better than to say 'I told you so' when I showed him the purple welts on my bottom. Instead, he repeated the more outrageous bits he remembered from the notebooks and laughed, till I began to laugh too.

'Will you go away when the British leave India?' Azhar asked me one day.

'I don't think so,' I said. 'My stepfather is Indian. My mother's family have lived here for generations.'

'Everyone is saying they're going to divide the country. I think I'll have to go away.'

'Oh, it won't happen,' I said glibly. 'How can they cut up such a big country?'

'Gandhi will stop them,' he said.

But even as we dismissed the possibility, Jinnah, Nehru and Mountbatten and all those who mattered were preparing their instruments for major surgery.

Before their decision had any effect on our life, we found a little freedom of our own—in an underground tunnel that we discovered in a corner of the school grounds. It was really part of an old, disused drainage system, and when Azhar and I began exploring it, we had no idea just how far it extended. After crawling along on our bellies for some twenty feet, we found ourselves in complete darkness. It was a bit frightening, but moving backwards would have been quite impossible, so we continued writhing forward, until we saw a glimmer of light at the end of the tunnel. Dusty, a little bruised and very scruffy, we emerged at last on to a grassy knoll, a little way outside the school boundary. We'd found a way to escape school!

The tunnel became our beautiful secret. We would sit and chat in it, or crawl through it just for the thrill of stealing out of the school to walk in the wilderness. Or to lie on the grass, our heads touching, reading comics or watching the kites and eagles wheeling in the sky. In those quiet moments, I became aware of the beauty and solace of nature more keenly than I had been till then: the scent of pine needles, the soothing calls of the Himalayan bulbuls, the feel of grass on bare feet, and the low music of the cicadas.

World War II had just come to an end, the United Nations held out the promise of a world living in peace and harmony, and India, an equal partner with Britain, would be among the great nations...

But soon we learnt that Bengal and Punjab provinces, with their large Muslim populations, were to be bisected. Everyone was in a hurry: Jinnah and company were in a hurry to get a country of their own; Nehru, Patel and others were in a hurry to run a free, if truncated, India; and Britain was in a hurry to get out. Riots flared up across northern India.

At school, the common room radio and the occasional newspaper kept us abreast of events. But in our tunnel Azhar and I felt immune from all that was happening, worlds away from all the pillage, murder and revenge. Outside the tunnel, there was fresh untrodden grass, sprinkled with clover and daisies, the only sounds the hammering of a woodpecker, and the distant insistent call of the Himalayan barbet. Who could touch us there?

'And when all wars are done,' I said, 'a butterfly will still be beautiful.'

'Did you read that somewhere?' Azhar asked.

'No, it just came into my head.'

'It's good. Already you're a writer.'

Though it felt good to hear him say that, I made light of it. 'No, I want to play hockey for India or football for Arsenal. Only winning teams!'

'You'll lose sometimes, you know, even if you get into those teams,' said wise old Azhar. 'You can't win forever. Better to be a writer.'

One morning after chapel, the headmaster announced that the Muslim boys—those who had their homes in what was now Pakistan—would have to be evacuated. They would be sent to their homes across the border with an armed convoy.

It was time for Azhar to leave, along with some fifty other boys from Lahore, Rawalpindi and Peshawar. The rest of us—Hindus, Christians, Buddhists, Sikhs and Parsis—helped them load their luggage into the waiting British Army trucks that would take them to Lahore. A couple of boys broke down and wept, including our departing school captain, a Pathan who had been known for his unemotional demeanour. Azhar waved to me and I waved back. We had vowed to meet again some day. We both kept our composure.

The headmaster announced a couple of days later that all the boys had reached Pakistan and were safe. On the morning of 15 August 1947, we were marched up to town to witness the Indian flag being raised for the first time. Shimla was still the summer capital of India, so it was quite an event. It was raining that morning. We were in our raincoats and gumboots, while a sea of umbrellas covered the Mall.

I was still a boy and did not think much of countries and nations, but what I did feel strongly about was the senseless division of the country that had separated me from my friends. Towards the end of the school year, just as I was getting ready to leave for Dehradun for the three-month winter holidays, I received a letter from Azhar. He told me something about his new school and how he missed my company and our games and our tunnel to freedom. I replied and gave him my home address, but I did not hear from him again. Perhaps the letters were lost, for there were many new borders. Even without those borders, the land, though divided, was still a big one, and we were very small.

Eighteen years later, I did get some news, but in an entirely different context. India and Pakistan were at war and in a bombing raid over Ambala, a Pakistani plane was shot down. An old school friend wrote to say he had heard the pilot's name was Azhar, but he couldn't be sure if it was the Azhar we knew.

Books and Friends

Now, during the school holidays, I came to Dehradun where my mother and stepfather lived with my siblings—my sister (back from Calcutta) and younger brother—and half siblings. Left largely to my own devices, I got into the habit of taking long walks, usually into the fields or tea-gardens on the outskirts of Dehra. I had no friends, but I must have been wanting some. One day, I went down to the railway tracks near the forest when a train was expected, and stood there, watching the carriages clatter past. Suddenly, a boy sitting at a carriage window waved and called out: 'Hey! Hello!' I kept looking at him till the train had gone. The next few days, I went to the same spot, expecting to see him again so that I could wave back, and maybe run alongside his carriage and ask his name and arrange to meet somewhere.

On one of my aimless walks I ended up at Granny's house, and asked her if there were any books lying around that I could read. I had never seen her reading a book; but there was always a chance that there would be something tucked away. Books do sometimes turn up in unexpected places. She gave me a religious tract, and told me to read it carefully.

Never despair has always been my motto, and I called on Granny's tenant next, with the same request. Miss Kellner occupied half the bungalow. She was a tiny, crippled spinster in her sixties, who had to be carried about by boys in livery and bathed by her ayah. My interaction with her till then had been limited to the occasional greeting, or a couple of sentences exchanged if we happened to be in the garden at the same time. Most of the time she was in fairly good spirits, despite her condition.

Usually she sat out in the garden, in an easy chair, in the shade of a pomelo tree.

'Do you have anything I can read, Miss Kellner?' I asked.

She was peering into a notebook. She looked up, and looked at me over her pince-nez glasses. 'Yes,' she said, and gave me a religious tract.

Apparently religious tracts were all the rage.

But hers came with a meringue and a soft nankhatai biscuit (made by a little bakery down the road), so I promised to read the tract.

Dropping in on Miss Kellner for a chat (and a snack) soon became a ritual of sorts, and I would turn up once a week, even by-passing

Granny on one or two occasions. I would also play cards with her—simple games like 'Swap' or 'Beggar-my-neighbour'; the only time in my life when I had the patience for card games. It's surprising what a well-stocked larder will do when it comes to making friends with a small boy.

So there she was—my first adult friend after my father's death—an ageing lady with a shattered spine, twisted hands, a very large nose (which seemed to suit her) and a frail, bent-double body. I seldom saw her out of her chair, except when she was being carried into or out of the house by her helpers. She was always neatly dressed, and I believe the morning bath courtesy her ayah was a ritual she never missed. All her close relatives had over the years passed away, and she was very much on her own. But her late parents had left her some money, which she seemed to manage quite well, employing the ayah, a cook and four boys whose job it was to carry her into the garden and back. When she needed to go out of the house, the boys carried her in a sedan chair, and when she went into town or to visit her friends for bridge parties, they took her around in her private sky-blue rickshaw. She was feather-light, and she kept the boys well fed, so the rickshaw flew down the road, and I think I once saw her clap her small hands in delight.

In spite of her infirmities, Miss Kellner had a healthy complexion and a good appetite. There was a story going around that she bathed in rosewater. I couldn't be so familiar as to ask her if this was true, but I decided to question her ayah on the subject. From my Jamnagar days, I usually got on well with ayahs, and they were fountains of gossip.

'Tell me, ayah-ji, does Miss Kellner really bathe in rosewater?' I asked quite innocently one day.

'None of your business,' snapped her loyal ayah. 'And what do you bathe in, inquisitive boy?'

'Donkey's milk,' I said mischievously, and allowed her to chase me around the pomelo tree.

I couldn't ask Miss Kellner about her disability, either. It was my mother who told me that when Miss Kellner was a baby, some fond uncle had been tossing her high in the air and catching her, when he was distracted by something and dropped her. The fall broke her spine, and her limbs, which never set properly. She had been an invalid ever since.

But mentally she was very alert. She would do her hisaab—accounts—in a large notebook, and though her hands were crooked, she would correspond with friends or distant relatives (I never found out who they were or where). She had a front room filled with all kinds of bric-a-brac she had collected over the years, and she would get her staff to dust and polish it every once in a while.

Soon enough, her ayah grew a little fond of me too. After we had talked for some time and played card games, Miss Kellner would say, 'You must be hungry', and I'd immediately say 'Yes', and she'd call the ayah, who knew exactly what was needed and would come with the meringues, patties and nankhatais.

I was the only child who would sit and talk to Miss Kellner. It wasn't just the meringues she gave me! I found her interesting, and oddly comforting. She had time for me, as I had time for her. In fact, she looked forward to my visits, which was not something I experienced anymore. I continued to spend time with Miss Kellner during my holidays for the next five or six years, and sometimes she wrote me cards when I was back at school in Shimla. Miss Kellner lived in the bungalow till she died in the early 1950s.

There was another friend I made in Granny's garden. Granny kept a gardener, Dhuki, a quiet man, who could have been forty, or sixty—I don't think anyone knew. He spent almost the entire day on his haunches, weeding the flower beds with the little spade, or khurpi, that he carried around. Dandelions, daisies, thistles, and other 'weeds' received no mercy from that relentless khurpi. Even some common marigolds flew from his spade.

'Don't throw those away,' I protested one day. 'They're so pretty!'

'Your grandmother doesn't like them,' said Dhuki.

In their place came petunias, poppies, sweet-peas, larkspur, snapdragons.

I liked the snapdragons. They came in many colours. And the sweet-peas gave out a heady fragrance. I think Granny grew most of her flowers for the sake of their fragrance. She could be unsmiling most of the time, but at least the garden was a friendly place. And Crazy, the dog, was still there. Now older and sleepier, but he still hated the postman. I was now too old to play hide and seek with him, though sometimes when he looked at me hopefully, I would oblige him by standing behind a tree trunk almost in plain sight. He would come up sniffing and waddling and find me and push his nose into my hands. He knew there would be a biscuit or two there for him. At all other times we just sat quietly next to each other and I would read him a comic or tell him a story that I wanted to write. Crazy was my kindest critic ever—a gentle snore would be his harshest criticism of a story that had gone on for too long.

When there was no other place to go to or people to visit, I stayed home with my siblings. Once in a while my mother and stepfather would remember my presence and we would have a few words to say to each other.

'Ruskin, we are leaving now. Are you sure you want to stay behind?'

'Uh-huh.'

'You are going to miss all the fun, child. And do look up from the book when someone is speaking to you.'

'I'll be fine. Don't worry.'

'In that case, bye, and wish us luck!'

'Good luck...to the poor animals.'

The last part of the last sentence I said in a whisper, or maybe not even a whisper but only in my mind. My mother and her husband were keen on shikar, or hunting, and would often be part of various hunting parties that went into the forests around Dehra and further afield, where they would train their guns on deer, nilgai, cheetal. But what they dreamt about was shooting a tiger.

I, on the other hand, had my sympathies firmly in place for the animals of the forest. A deer or chital, its ears twitching, its legs trembling as it prepared to take flight at the slightest hint of danger, and then the beautiful and graceful leap as it bounded into the depths of the forest—what could be more beautiful? Why would anyone want to shoot these lovely, harmless creatures for pleasure?

I did relent on one occasion, only to get away from my loud and mischievous brothers, and accompanied my mother, stepfather and some of their friends on a shikar trip. But I was determined to stay far away from all the guns and shooting. When the hunting party clambered into a jeep to drive into the forest for game, I refused to join them. Fortunately, the forest rest house had a shelf full of assorted books that seemed to have been forgotten by almost everyone. Here I discovered P.G. Wodehouse's *Love Among the Chickens*, M.R. James's *Ghost Stories of an Antiquary*, Agatha Christie's *Death on the Nile* and *Murder at the Vicarage*, A.A. Milne's *The Red House Mystery*, and *Sketches by Boz*, a collection of Dickens's short pieces.

I am glad to report now that at the shikar itself, nobody shot anything, the resident tiger having failed to appear, and the deer and nilgai having proved too swift for the hunters. I spent the two days reading, sometimes by a window and sometimes on the veranda, my only company the sleepy old cook, the occasional bird, the buzzing insects and a couple of friendly squirrels. It was the best possible way to spend time in a jungle. Just before evening on the second day, as I finished one P.G. Wodehouse and picked up another, I noticed a procession of small animals run by the rest house. Perhaps they were being driven out by the shikar party. There were deer and nilgai and peacocks. And then right before my astonished eyes, a leopard, deep black spots on flaming yellow, slunk quietly into view. It looked around warily, its tail swishing nervously. It crouched, and I could swear it looked straight at me once. Then it turned away disinterestedly and melted into the trees.

'Ruskin, you missed such an exciting day in the forest,' my mother said when the shikar expedition returned, empty-handed.

'Did I?'

'Yes, we saw so many animals. Pity none of us got a single one, though. We heard a leopard was on the prowl and we went all over the area trying to track it. But it got away.'

'That's good... I mean, that's sad.'

'And what did you do?'

'I read. And I saw a leopard.'

Of course, no one even believed me. But the incident made me a lifelong fan of leopards and Wodehouse.

~ 10 ~

Magic Eggs

Who doesn't like a magic show? Young or old, whatever the age, everyone sits up in happy anticipation upon hearing the words 'abracadabra' or '*chhoo mantar*'—or, as I was hearing now, 'gali-gali-gali'. I was ten years old and watching the famous magician Gogia Pasha do his act. He owned a café called Casino in Dehra. He would do a magic show here in the evenings, to get the crowd in. Later, the café would turn into a nightclub where there

would be plenty of dancing. Dehra in 1944-45 was a lively place. The town had been designated a rest and recreation centre for Allied troops, and it was full of soldiers on a break from active war duty in Burma and the Far East, all of them determined to have a good time. As a result, many restaurants and clubs had sprung up in downtown Dehradun.

I had discovered the Casino thanks to Irene. She was an eighteen-year-old Anglo-Indian girl who had taken a liking to me and would often take me with her when she went into town. She was tall and beautiful and very fashionable, and I had a big crush on her. She and I went to the Casino on a couple of occasions to watch Gogia Pasha make a rope dance and rise to the roof or make cards appear and disappear at will from a pack. Irene had promised that I could accompany her to Casino on New Year's Day, and I was so eager to be there, a few nights before I had a vivid dream that I remember even now in great detail. I saw that Gogia Pasha was on the stage. Suddenly his eyes fell on me and he beckoned.

'*Aa jao bachhe.* Come, come,' he called.

I hated being in the limelight, but there was no escape now. Irene, too, had a smile on her red lips and was gently encouraging me to step up. Reluctantly, I walked up to Pasha, who was dressed in a parrot-green robe and a red turban that would have suited a medieval sultan. Up close, I noticed he had dark, piercing eyes, thin lips and very hairy ears. He was certainly not a magician I would like to meet alone in a dark alley. But now he only smiled and gripping my shoulders with strong fingers turned me around to face the audience. Then, without any warning, he launched into a long spell of nonsensical words. '*Gali gali aa jaa aajaaa, chhoo mantar aajaa gali gali gali...*' I felt a whooshing noise inside my ears and to the sound of thunderous applause, I found that Pasha had extracted an egg, a coin and a ribbon from my left ear. I put in a finger and rubbed my ear in amazement. The crowd was going mad and I saw Irene clapping loudest of all. This magician act was certainly making me look good!

I now lost all my nervousness and was a willing stooge for Gogia Pasha. He ruffled my hair and made a full-grown pigeon appear. It sat on my head for a minute before fluttering away in a flurry of feathers. Then Pasha asked me to lie down on a table and pulled out a tin sword from his robe. He announced he was going to cut me in half. I think he had hypnotized me, because I said not a word in protest. 'Worry not, my *chhota dost*,' he whispered to me. For a moment I gave a thought to my mother and school friends and Irene, and wondered what would happen if I was never put together again. But not for nothing was Gogia Pasha called the Master of Magic. Sawed in half I was, and then put together as well as before. There was wild applause and Irene called me her brave little boy! It was all such a pleasant dream that I have never forgotten it.

On the evening the year 1944 drew to a close, Irene let me stay on with her late into the night. She had permission from my mother and stepfather, who were always encouraging me to have some fun. The club filled up as the night rolled on and everyone was in high spirits, dancing to the latest Hollywood songs. I remember taking a few sips from Irene's strong brown-coloured drink, and feeling very pleasantly dizzy! Finally, she ordered a plate of fish fingers for me and a glass of Vimto while she went on the dance floor with a smart English soldier. I sulked in my corner and was quite upset at this turn of events. But as the clock struck midnight and the hall exploded into 'Auld Lang Syne' to welcome

the new year, Irene returned to give me a hug and a special kiss. Then, making my new year's wish come true, she swept me up with her and we danced a quick foxtrot. I didn't know a foxtrot from a tango, but it did not matter. Irene was a wonderful dancer, and with her in the lead, I felt like the most graceful person in the room. When we walked back home that night, in my heart I was still dancing. Maybe this was a different kind of magic, one that I was just beginning to understand.

And the magic time wasn't over yet. Two days later, it snowed in Dehra. I was out walking when it began. It came down quite suddenly, and soon the litchi and guava trees were covered with a soft mantle of snow. I vividly remember running in and telling my mother, 'It's snowing outside, Mum!' and she said, 'I don't want any of your silly jokes right now, Ruskin,' because she had just given birth to my second half-brother, and was in bed.

So I ran out and came back with some litchi leaves which were covered with snow, and her face lit up with a delighted smile.

Later Miss Kellner told me it had snowed in Dehradun once before, forty years earlier, when she first came here.

'Now maybe it's a sign that I should go,' she said.

'Don't go,' I said. 'Wait for the next snowfall.'

This pleased her, and we played Snap. The ayah brought us ginger biscuits, and I polished them all off and asked for more.

~

And so, life fell into another pattern. Holidays would be spent in Dehra with my mother, stepfather and siblings, and I would visit Granny and Miss Kellner often. I even made a few friends during my long walks around the town. The manager of the only movie hall in town showing English movies became a friend, as did a bunch of local boys, among them the tall and scrappy Haripal, an outgoing and energetic Sikh boy with whom I played football.

The rest of the year I would be in school in Shimla. Here, the library became my retreat and harbour. A kind teacher had put me in charge of the library. I had the keys, and would go there at odd hours, saying I would catalogue the books but, in reality, to pore over them and become familiar with many well-known names as well as some obscure ones. Over the years I read Dickens, Stevenson, Jack London, H.G. Wells, J.B. Priestley, the Brontë sisters, Somerset Maugham and Ben Travers; the complete plays of J.M. Barrie and Bernard Shaw; and the essays—a form that I have always liked—of A.G. Gardiner, Belloc, Chesterton and many others. And then, of course, there were the humorous writers—Mark Twain, Thurber,

Wodehouse, Stephen Leacock, Jerome K. Jerome, Barry Pain, Damon Runyon—and George and Weedon Grossmith, whose *The Diary of a Nobody* remains my favourite humorous book. My own life being somewhat dull, it was good to lose myself in the worlds conjured up by these writers.

The best place in school after the library was the common room. Every house had a junior and a senior common room. These came up in my final two years in school. Here you could relax in comfortable chairs—there were books to read, and there was a radio, and we were encouraged to listen to the news and the cricket or football commentaries.

I was no longer so young that I would be made to sit in a corner with a plate of fish fingers and a fizzy soft drink while others did the dancing. By the final year of school, one of the most anticipated social events was the annual dance. The senior boys were taken to

Auckland House where we could chat with the Auckland House girls, and dance with them. I danced with a girl called Indu in 1949–50. She was a princess from Jazdan, a tiny princely state in Kathiawar, very close to where I had lived as a little boy. Perhaps we had even met as infants at one of the Jam Sahib's parties in Jamnagar and fate had brought us together again—who is to tell? And we met again as oldies over half a century later—she dropped in one day, grey-haired, still slim (I was not) and smart and very charming, and we spent a pleasant evening talking about schooldays and dances and lost friends.

I remember writing Indu a letter after our first dance. It was intercepted by her headmistress or some other teacher and it was sent to my headmaster, a person who had no affection for me at all. I did get into a bit of trouble, but one result of that episode was that I became popular, and was sought after by some of the boys who wanted me to write similar letters for them. Some years later, when I was in Dehradun after school, I wrote many love letters for the boys and young men there. They didn't care for my stories, but they would come to me to get their love letters and job applications written!

A Boy's Own Room

My sixteenth birthday came and went and I was finished with my final school exams. Despite some ill health, I did fairly well and left school forever, more with a sense of relief than nostalgia. I came to live with my mother and the family in Dehra. And I soon discovered that being in the same house as everyone else all the time would take some getting used to.

One day, after an argument with my mother over the playing of the radio, I walked out of the house in a huff. I would never return, I declared, and I truly meant it. I was determined to find my own place to live, no matter what. However, I soon discovered that this is a bit difficult when one is sixteen and with no money. I spent a few days with a friend, and then swallowed my pride and returned home! My mother said nothing, but she would have understood my feelings, because soon afterwards, I was given a separate room of my own—a small room on the roof, or a barsati.

My tiny barsati opened on to the flat concrete roof of the building. There was no other construction on the roof, and a flight of stone steps ran up to it on the outside of the building, so it was quite private. I lived more or less independent of my family—I saw them two or three times a day when I went down for my meals. My steps were steep and people seldom came up to see me, the exceptions being the inquisitive boys of the neighbourhood.

There was a banyan tree just opposite. Squirrels were busy in it all afternoon, sparrows, crows and other birds in the morning and evening, and flying foxes at night. This was the first time I'd had a room with a view all to myself, and I think this was when I really began responding to the sights, smells, colours and everyday theatre of the world around me.

A broad path ran beside the building which wasn't very busy, but the activity on it was always interesting: a 'boxwallah', with a tin trunk on his head, selling everything from bread and biscuits from the bakeries to hair oil, safety pins and elastic for pyjamas; an ayah with a baby in a pram; the rent-collector, with the teeth and nostrils of a horse; the postman on his brand new Atlas bicycle; the fruit-seller calling his wares in high-pitched, rather eccentric cries; a line of schoolgirls with red ribbons in their pigtails.

When it rained, there was greater activity. At the first rumblings, women would rush outside to bring in the washing—and if there was a strong breeze, to chase a few garments across the compound. When the rain came, it came with a vengeance, making a muddy river of the path. A cyclist would come riding furiously down the path, shoulders hunched and head bent low; an elderly gentleman would be having difficulty keeping a large umbrella above his head; naked children would be squealing and dancing about in the downpour.

I had a window and two doors. One door was at the top of a flight of twenty-two steps by which I entered the room (by an odd coincidence, my present abode, Ivy Cottage, also has twenty-two steps leading up to the front door). Another door opened on to the flat, cemented roof of the building. It was hot by the end of April, and as I had no fan I kept

the doors and windows open day and night to let in whatever breeze might be coming down from the hills. Sometimes it was a hot wind from Delhi, but occasionally the wind came off the Tibetan plateau and the distant snows to provide a little relief from the soaring temperatures.

Open doors and windows meant easy access for birds and other small creatures. A pair of noisy mynahs—one of them bald after a fight—were frequently in and out of the room, paying no attention to me as I sat at my desk or lay supine on my bed in vest and shorts. Sparrows were resting in the little skylight, and I dared not open it, for fear of knocking down their rather precarious abode. A chameleon circled the terrace in search of lost friends, and sometimes raised its head to look in from the threshold.

I would leave the front door open, even at night. But late one night, I was woken from deep sleep by a hideous howling right next to my bed. Switching on the light, I found a jackal right beside me, baying at the moon or the stars or some lost love on the rooftops. I gave a shout and it ran away, down the steps and across the road, hotly pursued by all the dogs in the area barking furiously. I expect the poor jackal had received a bigger fright than I had; but after that, I kept the front door closed at night.

But during the day the door was always open, and through it, one morning, came a light-eyed Sikh boy of about twelve, as yet unbearded, wearing khaki shorts and chappals, looking at me as if I were an exotic and endangered bird. Then he laughed, and it was like a shower of rain on a hot summer day.

This was Somi, whom I'd met briefly at his brother Haripal's house. Haripal was fifteen, studying in the tenth standard, after which he wanted to join the army or navy—which did not impress me, because I had a low opinion of regimentation of any kind. I told him I wanted to be a writer—which did not impress him, because that was not a career, he said, and in any case, that sort of thing was possible only in England or America, and I was in India.

Haripal took me home for lunch one day, and it was there I met his mother, who made me welcome, and his brothers Somi and Chhotu and his cousins Dipi and Daljit. Their home was on the outskirts of the town, where civilization began to merge with the jungle. It was the first of the few large families I would attach myself to over the years, and they were all kind enough to put up with me, letting me come and go as I pleased.

After that first visit, when he came wanting help with English lessons—which were soon forgotten—Somi would turn up at odd hours. Soon, we were laying out a roof garden. Somi played truant from school and we spent two days carrying up mud in a bucket from a nearby field. By the evening of the second day, we had laid out a neat little flower bed. Somi and Chhotu buried some pumpkin seeds in it, though I would have preferred flowers, and we had a little argument about this and later made up by going out to eat chaat.

Many were the afternoons we spent lazing around and chatting in that room. But it was cycling that Somi enjoyed most of all. I wasn't much of a bicycle rider; I was always falling off, and once went sailing into a buffalo cart and fractured my arm. But it was fun being with Somi and his brothers, and I would hire an old bicycle from a cycle-hire shop and accompany them on rides in the hot sun—sometimes to the sulphur springs, or to Premnagar (where the Military Academy was situated), or into the tea gardens along the Haridwar road, or across the dry riverbed at Lachhiwala and into the forest. We would spend hours sitting by the canal and discuss our hopes and dreams.

Everyone wanted to go away. Dehra was too small for our ambitions, and at that age we all wanted to conquer the world. My dream—to be a writer—could only be realized in England, where, I believed, the doors of the literary world would open for me.

After the long cycle rides, we would end up in my room, tired and thirsty. I had started writing stories and sending them to magazines and newspapers. Only *My Magazine of India* had published these and even sent me a few money orders as payments. With these I splurged on ices and cold drinks. Those money orders helped me make a bit of an event of my seventeenth birthday—for the first time in my life, I celebrated with a party. Six boys, some crows and a dog (Chhotu's pet) feasted on samosas, ice cream (homemade, from blancmange powder), lemonade and Indian mithaais and English confectionery, served in plates and tumblers borrowed from the neighbours. Chhotu and Somi got the most to eat because one was the youngest and the other the most loving and good-looking of the gang.

The days were slipping by like this—and I was recording them in a journal, mainly about my dear and new friends—until it was finally decided that I would go to England. My aunt lived in the Jersey islands, and I would go live with her there, learn some occupation, and make a living. In my heart, I knew this was my first step to becoming a writer.

My passage was booked on the P & O liner S.S. *Strathnaver*, one of several smart passenger ships that plied between Bombay and London; or rather, Sydney and London, because it began its voyage in Australia. My ticket arrived. It cost Rs 450, which included meals on the ship. The voyage would last just over a fortnight. The ticket and some clothes and a few other belongings for my early days in England were bought with some money that Dehra Granny had left me in her will. She did not have much, but she had thought of me. She hadn't told me, and up until now my mother hadn't either, and now stern old Granny wasn't around for me to thank her—

she had died when I was still at boarding school in Shimla.

As the day for my departure to England approached, I began to panic at the thought of leaving, and an old feeling of loneliness returned. Leaving my family wasn't the hardest part; it was the friends I had made that I would miss the most. But I was clumsy at expressing my feelings, as were most of the other boys—except Somi, always frank and spontaneous in his affection.

'I will be sad, Ruskin,' he said simply.

'I'll come back,' I said.

'You won't. You will forget us.'

A week later he was ill with pneumonia. I didn't think I could leave, but Haripal, always pragmatic, told me not to worry. Somi would get well soon enough, but I would lose my only chance to do what I'd always wanted to do. My staying wouldn't help.

And Somi willed himself to health, as if

he was determined to send me off without guilt or worry. His mother took me aside the last time I went to their home. 'Do you need anything, son?' she asked. 'You belong to this family, you must tell me if there's anything you need.'

She took my face in her hands and I broke down. 'Be brave,' she whispered, and kissed my forehead.

It was early November of 1951 when I left Dehra. My mother and stepfather came to the station to see me off. My friends were also at the station to see me off. Somi and his brothers, Krishan and Ranbir. So it was quite a jolly affair in the end. No tears, no regrets. Everyone admired me for going off on my own while still a minor.

'You're going to be a great writer,' pronounced Krishan. 'Best in the world!'

How I loved those loving boys, now being left behind in a small town called Dehradun, unheard of outside India back then, while I set off for the famous land of Dickens and Buckingham Palace!

The train set off for Bombay, and as I looked out of the window and saw my young friends standing there on the platform, waving and cheering, I knew I was saying goodbye to my own boyhood and to theirs, and that if I ever saw them again we would all be grown men, the days of innocence far behind us.

Somi ran beside the carriage, shouting goodbye, and laughing as he ran, tears streaming down his face.

It was decades before I met Somi again—he was on a visit from America, where he had settled. A silver-haired man, father of married children. And I was even older! But in my mind Somi remains an eternal innocent, a boy in shorts, his turban slightly askew, riding his bicycle down an empty road. In that image lies all that is beautiful about my boyhood, a time of light and shade and light again that I shall never forget.

Epilogue

I came back to India after four and a half years in England. I knew where I belonged, and where I would live for the rest of my life.

Another ship brought me to Bombay, and from Bombay I took the train to Delhi and then to Dehradun. As the train approached Dehra, it entered a forest of familiar green. Every click of the rails brought me closer to all that I had missed and was now coming back to reclaim as my own. I belonged to the hot sunshine and muddy canals, the banyan trees and the mango groves, the smell of wet earth after summer rain, the relief of a monsoon thunderstorm, the laughing brown faces, the strangers who very quickly became dear friends. I missed everything that made it all right to be sentimental and emotional.

In Dehra, Somi's cousin Dipi was at the station with his bicycle. I put my suitcase and travel bag in my stepfather's second-hand car, pulled myself onto the crossbar of Dipi's bicycle, and we rode through the streets of the town that had shaped my life, and brought me home.

In England, I had written a book, *The Room on the Roof*, based on my last year in Dehra, spent in that room on the roof with Somi, Krishan, Haripal and other friends. The book had been accepted, after many rejections, by the publisher Andre Deutsche. However, till

I left, I had no idea what had become of it. Perhaps it would never see the light of day. Nevertheless, in Dehra now, I started anew, sending stories to magazines all over India. The average payment was about twenty-five rupees a story. Ten stories a month would therefore fetch me two hundred and fifty rupees—just enough for me to get by.

Only *The Illustrated Weekly of India*, a leading paper of the day, paid Rs 50 per story, and fortunately quite a few of my stories appeared in the paper. One day, a letter from the editor Shaun Mandy informed me that he was going to serialize *The Room on the Roof*—and that was how I knew it had been published in England. Copies of the book finally turned up in the post, but I first saw my debut book in print when serialization began in the *Weekly*, with lively illustrations by Mario Miranda, the *Weekly*'s well-known cartoonist and illustrator. That was in 1956, and I recall the morning well, because I wrote about it soon afterwards. I was twenty-two then and I am eighty-four now; a lot has happened since then, and if I sat down to make a list of all my mornings, I would probably remember more eventful ones. But as it was my first book, I suppose it deserves commemoration, so here's the piece I wrote:

> *I was up a little earlier than usual, well before sunrise, well before my landlady, Bibiji, called up to me to come down for my tea and parathas. It was going to be a special day and I wanted to tell the world about it. But when you're twenty-one, the world isn't really listening to you.*
>
> *I bathed at the tap, put on a clean (but unpressed) shirt, trousers that needed cleaning, shoes that needed polishing. I never cared much about appearances. But I did have a nice leather belt with studs! I tightened it to the last notch. I was a slim boy, just a little undernourished.*

On the streets, the milkmen on their bicycles were making their rounds, reminding me of William Saroyan, who sold newspapers as a boy, and recounted his experiences in The Bicycle Rider in Beverley Hills. Stray dogs and cows were nosing at dustbins. A truck loaded with bananas was slowly making its way towards the mandi. In the distance there was the whistle of an approaching train.

One or two small tea shops had just opened, and I stopped at one of them for a cup of tea. As it was a special day, I decided to treat myself to an omelette. The shopkeeper placed a record on his new electric record player, and the strains of a popular film tune served to wake up all the neighbours—a song about a girl's red dupatta being blown away by a gust of wind and then retrieved by a handsome but unemployed youth. I finished my omelette and set off down the road to the bazaar.

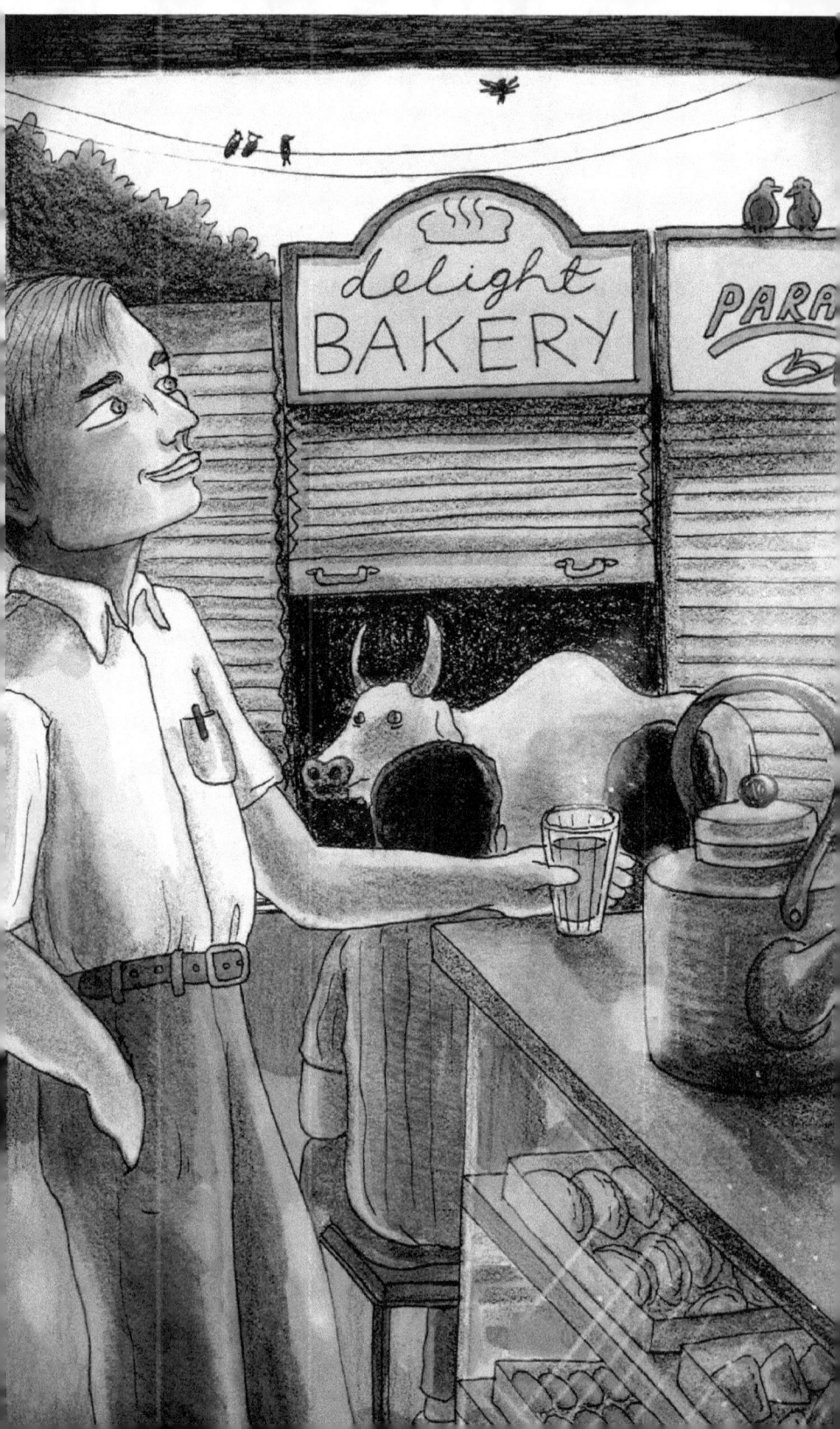

It was a little too early for most of the shops to be open, but the news agency would be the first and that was where I was heading.

And there it was: the National News Agency, with piles of fresh newspapers piled up at the entrance. The Leader of Allahabad, the Pioneer of Lucknow, the Tribune of Ambala, and the bigger national dailies. But where was the latest Illustrated Weekly of India? Was it late this week? I did not always get up at six in the morning to pick up the Weekly, but this week's issue was a special one. It was my issue, my special bow to the readers of India and the whole wide beautiful wonderful world. My novel was to be published in England, but first it would be serialized in India!

Mr Gupta popped his head out of the half-open shop door and smiled at me.

'What brings you here so early this morning?'

'Has the Weekly arrived?'

'Come in. It's here. I can't leave it on the pavement'.

I produced a rupee. 'Give me two copies.'

'Something special in it? Did you win first prize in the crossword competition?'

My hands were not exactly trembling as I opened the magazine, but my heart was in my mouth as I flipped through the pages of that revered journal—the one and only family magazine of the 1950s, the gateway to literary success—edited by a quirky Irishman, Shaun Mandy.

And there it was: the first instalment of The Room on the Roof, that naïve, youthful novel on which I had toiled for a couple of years. It had lively, evocative illustrations by Mario, who wasn't much older than me. And a picture of the young author, looking gauche and gaunt and far from intellectual.

I waved the magazine in front of Mr Gupta. 'My novel!' I told him. 'In this and the next five issues!'

He wasn't too impressed. 'Well, I hope circulation won't drop,' he laughed. 'And you should have sent them a better photograph.'

Expansively, I bought a third copy.

'Circulation is going up!' said Mr Gupta.

The bazaar was slowly coming to life.

Spring was in the air, and there was a spring in my step as I sauntered down the road. I wanted to tell the world about my triumph, but was the world interested? I had no mentors in our sleepy little town. There was no one to whom I could go and confide: 'Look what I've done. And it was all due to your encouragement, thanks!' Because there hadn't been anyone to encourage or help, not then nor in the receding past. The members of the local cricket team, among whom I had friends, would certainly be interested, and one or two would exclaim: 'Shabash! Now you can get us some new pads!' And there were other friends who would demand a party at the chaat shop, which was fine, but would any of them read my book?

But perhaps one or two would read it, out of loyalty.

A cow stood in the middle of the road, blocking my way.

'See here, friend cow,' I said, displaying the magazine to the ruminating animal. *'Here's the first instalment of my novel. What do you think of it?'*

The cow looked at the magazine with definite interest. Those crisp new pages looked good to eat. She craned forward as if to accept my offer of breakfast, but I snatched the magazine away.

'I'll lend it to you another day,' I said, and moved on.

A different phase of my life began after that. I was finally a writer—something I had always dreamed of becoming. Many, many years of struggle followed, and then some success. Many more friends came into my life and went out of it. I found a loving family. I grew up, grew old (or so I am told). But everything that gives meaning to my life—everything good and lasting and beautiful—has its origin in my early years. I may be everyone's favourite grandfather now—a grandfather who tells stories—but deep down I am, and shall always remain, the boy that I was.

My dear, gentle reader, may you also remain forever young.

Ruskin Bond was born in Kasauli in 1934, and grew up in Jamnagar, Dehradun, Delhi and Shimla. He lived in England for four years, returning to India in 1955. He is the author of over a hundred books of fiction, non-fiction and poetry. Among them are *The Room on the Roof*, *A Flight of Pigeons*, *The Night Train at Deoli*, *Time Stops at Shamli*, *The Blue Umbrella*, *Rain in the Mountains*, *A Book of Simple Living*, *Friends in Wild Places* and *Lone Fox Dancing*. He received the John Llewellyn Rhys Prize in 1956, the Sahitya Akademi Award in 1993, the Padma Shri in 1999 and the Padma Bhushan in 2014. He lives in Landour, Mussoorie with his adopted family.

Sunaina Coelho grew up in New Delhi and studied at the National Institute of Design, Ahmedabad. She currently lives in Kochi, with her husband Fahad Faizal and their baby boy.

She and Fahad have a company called Babakiki, where they create animated and illustrated products for various companies. In her free time she enjoys exploring cuisines, books and most importantly, the outdoors.

www.ingramcontent.com/pod-product-compliance
Lightning Source LLC
Chambersburg PA
CBHW061940220426
43662CB00012B/1975